London River

by

H. M. Tomlinson

London River
by H. M. Tomlinson

ISBN: 978-93-59326-59-7

Published by

DOUBLE 9 BOOKS

2/13-B, Ansari Road
Daryaganj, New Delhi – 110002
info@double9books.com
www.double9books.com
Tel. 011-40042856

ABOUT THE AUTHOR

H. M. (Henry Major) Tomlinson (1873-1958) was a British author, journalist, and travel writer recognized for his poetic and vibrant writing style. Tomlinson, he was born on June 21, 1873, in England's Surrey county, had an effective professional life encompassing numerous types of literature. Tomlinson began his career as a journalist for the London Evening Standard and The Observer. His early experiences as a sailor in the British merchant navy encouraged his writing as well, establishing a great love of the sea and nautical life that would be reflected in his works. He was well-known for his travel writing, that frequently focused on his travels to many regions of the world, including the South Seas, Africa, and Europe. His travel memoirs combined vivid descriptions, philosophical thoughts, and a keen sense of observation, resulting in works that were both informative and deeply meditative. "The Sea and the Jungle" (1912), a description of his travels in South America, is one of his important works. This book illustrates his ability to combine travelogue and reflection, capturing nature's majesty and volatility while diving into larger concerns of human existence.

CONTENTS

I
The Foreshore

It begins on the north side of the City, at Poverty Corner. It begins imperceptibly, and very likely is no more than what a native knows is there. It does not look like a foreshore. It looks like another of the byways of the capital. There is nothing to distinguish it from the rest of Fenchurch Street. You will not find it in the Directory, for its name is only a familiar bearing used by seamen among themselves. If a wayfarer came upon it from the west, he might stop to light a pipe (as well there as anywhere) and pass on, guessing nothing of what it is and of its memories. And why should he? London is built of such old shadows; and while we are here casting our own there is not much time to turn and question what they fall upon. Yet if some unreasonable doubt, a suspicion that he was being watched, made a stranger hesitate at that corner, he might begin to feel that London there was as different from Bayswater and Clapham as though deep water intervened. In a sense deep water does; and not only the sea, but legends of ships that have gone, and of the men who knew them, and traditions of a service older than anything Whitehall knows, though still as lively as enterprise itself, and as recent as the ships which moved on today's high water.

In a frame outside one of its shops hangs a photograph of a sailing ship. The portrait is so large and the beauty of the subject so evident that it might have been the cause of the stranger stopping there to fill his pipe. Yet how could he know that to those groups of men loitering about the name of that ship is as familiar as Suez or Rio, even though they have never seen her? They know her as well as they know their business. They know her house-flag—it is indistinguishable in the picture—and her master, and it is possible the oldest of them remembers the clippers of that fleet of which she alone now carries the emblem; for this is not only another year, but another era. But they do not look at her portrait. They spit into the road, or stare across it, and rarely move from where they stand, except to pace up and down as though keeping a watch. At one time, perhaps thirty years ago, it was usual to see gold rings in their ears. It is said that if you wanted a bunch of men to run a little river steamer, with a freeboard of six inches, out to Delagoa Bay, you could engage them all at this corner, or at the taverns just up the turning. The suggestion of such a voyage, in such a ship, would turn us to look on these men in wonder, for it is the way of all but the wise to expect appearance to betray admirable qualities. These fellows, though, are not significant, except that you might think of some of them that their ease and indifference were assumed, and that, when trying not to look so, they were very conscious of the haste and importance of this great city into which that corner jutted far enough for them. They have just landed, or they are about to sail again, and they might be standing on the shore eyeing the town beyond, in which the luck of ships is cast by strangers they never see, but who are inimical to them, and whose ways are inscrutable.

If there are any inland shops which can hold one longer than the place where that ship's portrait hangs, then I do not know them. That comes from no more, of course, than the usual fault of an early impression. That fault gives a mould to the mind, and our latest thoughts, which we try to make reasonable, betray that accidental shape. It may be said that I looked into this window while still soft. The consequence, everybody knows, would be incurable in a boy who saw sextants for the first time, compasses, patent logs, sounding-machines, signalling gear, and the other secrets of navigators. And not only those things. There was a section given to books, with classics like Stevens on *Stowage*, and Norie's *Navigation*, volumes never seen west of Gracechurch Street. The books were all for the eyes of sailors, and were sorted by chance. *Knots and Splices*, *Typee*, *Know Your Own Ship*, the *South Pacific Directory*, and *Castaway on the Auckland Islands*. There were many of them, and they were in that fortuitous and attractive order. The back of every volume had to be read, though the light was bad. On one wall between the windows a specimen chart was framed. Maps are good; but how much better are charts, especially when you cannot read them except by guessing at their cryptic lettering! About the coast line the fathom marks cluster thickly, and venture to sea in lines which attenuate, or become sparse clusters, till the chart is blank, being beyond soundings. At the capes are red dots, with arcs on the seaward side to show at what distance mariners pick up the real lights at night. Through such windows, boys with bills of lading and mates' receipts in their pockets, being on errands to shipowners, look outward, and only seem to look inward. Where are the confines of London?

Opposite Poverty Corner there is, or used to be, an archway into a courtyard where in one old office the walls were hung with half-models of sailing ships. I remember the name of one, the *Winefred*. Deed-boxes stood on shelves, with the name of a ship on each. There was a mahogany counter, an encrusted pewter inkstand, desks made secret with high screens, and a silence that might have been the reproof to intruders of a repute remembered in dignity behind the screens by those who kept waiting so unimportant a visitor as a boy. On the counter was a stand displaying sailing cards, announcing, among other events in London River, "the fine ship *Blackadder* for immediate dispatch, having most of her cargo engaged, to Brisbane." And in those days, just round the corner in Billiter Street, one of the East India Company's warehouses survived, a sombre relic among the new limestone and red granite offices, a massive archway in its centre leading, it could be believed, to an enclosure of night left by the eighteenth century, and forgotten. I never saw anybody go into it, or come out. How could they? It was of another time and place. The familiar Tower, the Guildhall that we knew nearly as well, the Cathedral which certainly existed, for it could often be seen in the distance, and the Abbey that was little more than something we had heard named, they were but the scenery close to the buses. Yet London was more wonderful than anything they could make it appear. About Fenchurch Street and Leadenhall Street wagons could be seen going east, bearing bales and cases, and the packages were port-marked for Sourabaya, Para, Ilo-Ilo, and Santos—names like those. They had to be seen to be believed. You could stand there, forced to think that the sun never did more than make the floor of asphalted streets glow like polished brass, and that the evening light was full of glittering motes and smelt of dust, and that life worked itself out in cupboards made of glass and mahogany; and suddenly you learned, while smelling the dust, that Acapulco was more than a portent in a book and held only by an act of faith. Yet that astonishing revelation, enough to make any youthful messenger forget where he himself was bound, through turning to follow with his eyes that acceptance by a carrier's cart of the verity of the fable, is nowhere mentioned, I have found since, in any guide to London, though you may learn how Cornhill got its name.

For though Londoners understand the Guildhall pigeons have as much right to the place as the aldermen, they look upon the seabirds by London Bridge as vagrant strangers. They do not know where their city ends on the east side. Their River descends from Oxford in more than one sense. It has little history worth mentioning below Westminster. To the poets, the River becomes flat and songless where at Richmond the sea's remote influence just moves it; and there they leave it. The Thames goes down then to a wide grey vacuity, a featureless monotony where men but toil, where life becomes silent in effort, and goes out through fogs to nowhere in particular. But there is a hill-top at Woolwich from which, better than from Richmond, our River, the burden-bearer, the road which joins us to New York and Sydney, can be seen for what it is, plainly related to a vaster world, with the ships upon its bright path moving through the smoke and buildings of the City. And surely some surmise of what our River is comes to a few of that multitude who cross London Bridge every day? They favour the east side of it, I have noticed, and they cannot always resist a pause to stare overside to the Pool. Why do they? Ships are there, it is true, but only insignificant traders, diminished by sombre cliffs up which their cargo is hauled piece-meal to vanish instantly into mid-air caverns; London absorbs all they have as morsels. Anyhow, it is the business of ships. The people on the bridge watch another life below, with its strange cries and mysterious movements. A leisurely wisp of steam rises from a steamer's funnel. She is alive and breathing, though motionless. The walls enclosing the Pool are spectral in a winter light, and might be no more than the almost forgotten memory of a dark past. Looking at them intently, to give them a name, the wayfarer on the bridge could imagine they were maintained there only by the frail effort of his will. Once they were, but now, in some moods, they are merely remembered. Only the men busy on the deck of the ship below are real. Through an arch beneath the feet a barge shoots out noiselessly on the ebb, and staring down at its sudden apparition you feel dizzily that it has the bridge in tow, and that all you people on it are being drawn unresisting into that lower world of shades. You release yourself from this spell with an effort, and look at the faces of those who are beside you at the parapet. What are their thoughts? Do they know? Have they also seen the ghosts? Have they felt stirring a secret and forgotten desire, old memories, tales that were told? They move away and go to their desks, or to their homes in the suburbs. A vessel that has hauled into the fairway calls for the Tower Bridge gates to be opened for her. She is going. We watch the eastern mists take her from us. For we never are so passive and well-disciplined to the things which compel us but rebellion comes at times—misgiving that there is a world beyond the one we know, regret that we never ventured and made no discovery, and that our time has been saved and not spent. The gates to the outer world close again.

There, where that ship vanished, is the highway which brought those unknown folk whose need created London out of reeds and mere. It is our oldest road, and now has many bypaths. Near Poverty Corner is a building which recently was dismissed with a brief, humorous reference in a new guide to our City—a cobbled forecourt, tame pigeons, cabs, a brick front topped by a clock-face: Fenchurch Street Station. Beyond its dingy platforms, the metal track which contracts into the murk is the road to China, though that is, perhaps, the last place you would guess to be at the end of it. The train runs over a wilderness of tiles, a grey plateau of bare slate and rock, its expanse cracked and scored as though by a withering heat. Nothing grows there; nothing could live there. Smoke still pours from it, as though it were volcanic, from numberless vents. The region is without sap. Above its expanse project superior fumaroles, their drifting vapours dissolving great areas. When the track descends slightly, you see cavities in that cliff which runs parallel with your track. The desert is actually burrowed, and every hole in the plateau is a habitation. Something does live there. That region of burnt and fissured rock is tunneled and inhabited. The unlikely serrations and ridges with the smoke moving over them are porous, and a fluid life ranges beneath unseen. It is the beginning of Dockland. That the life is in upright beings, each with independent volition and a soul; that it is not an amorphous movement, flowing in bulk through buried pipes, incapable of the idea of height, of rising, it is difficult to believe. It has not been believed. If life, you protest, is really there, has any purpose which is better than that of extending worm-like through the underground, then why, at intervals, is there not an upheaval, a geyser-like burst, a plain hint from a power usually pent, but liable to go skywards? But that is for the desert to answer. As by mocking chance the desert itself almost instantly shows what possibilities are hidden within it. The train roars unexpectedly over a viaduct, and below is a deep hollow filled with light, with a floor of water, and a surprise of ships. How did that white schooner get into such an enclosure? Is freedom nearer here than we thought?

The crust of roofs ends abruptly in a country which is a complexity of gasometers, canals, railway junctions, between which cabbage fields in long spokes radiate from the train and revolve. There is the grotesque suggestion of many ships in the distance, for through gaps in a nondescript horizon masts appear in a kaleidoscopic way. The journey ends, usually in the rain, among iron sheds that are topped on the far side by the rigging and smoke-stacks of great liners. There is no doubt about it now. At the corner of one shed, sheltering from the weather, is a group of brown men in coloured rags, first seen in the gloom because of the whites of their eyes. What we remember of such a day is that it was half of night, and the wind hummed in the cordage, and swayed wildly the loose gear aloft. Towering hulls were ranged down each side of a lagoon that ended in vacancy. The rigging and funnels of the fleet were unrelated; those ships were phantom and monstrous. They seemed on too great a scale to be within human control. We felt diminished and a little fearful, as among the looming urgencies of a dream. The forms were gigantic but vague, and they were seen in a smother of the elements; and their sounds, deep and mournful, were like the warnings of something alien, yet without form, which we knew was adverse, but could not recall when awake again. We remember, that day, a few watchers insecure on an exposed dockhead that projected into a sullen dreariness of river and mud which could have been the finish of the land. At the end of a creaking hawser was a steamer canting as she backed to head downstream—now she was exposed to a great adventure—the tide rapid and noisy on her plates, the reek from her funnel sinking over the water. And from the dockhead, in the fuddle of a rain-squall, we were waving a handkerchief, probably to the wrong man, till the vessel went out where all was one—rain, river, mud, and sky, and the future.

It is afterwards that so strange an ending to a brief journey from a City station is seen to have had more in it than the time-table, hurriedly scanned, gave away. Or it would be remembered as strange, if the one who had to make that journey as much as thought of it again; for perhaps to a stranger occupied with more important matters it was passed as being quite relevant to the occasion, ordinary and rather dismal, the usual boredom of a duty. Its strangeness depends, very likely, as much on an idle and squandering mind as on the ships, the River, and the gasometers. Yet suppose you first saw the River from Blackwall Stairs, in the days when the windows of the *Artichoke Tavern*, an ancient, weather-boarded house with benches outside, still looked towards the ships coming in! And how if then, one evening, you had seen a Blackwall liner haul out for the Antipodes while her crew sang a chanty! It might put another light on the River, but a light, I will admit, which others should not be expected to see, and if they looked for it now might not discover, for it is possible that it has vanished, like the old tavern. It is easy to persuade ourselves that a matter is made plain by the light in which we prefer to see it, for it is our light.

One day, I remember, a boy had to take a sheaf of documents to a vessel loading in the London Dock. She was sailing that tide. It was a hot July noon. It is unlucky to send a boy, who is marked by all the omens for a City prisoner, to that dock, for it is one of the best of its kind. He had not been there before. There was an astonishing vista, once inside the gates, of sherry butts and port casks. On the flagstones were pools of wine lees. There was an unforgettable smell. It was of wine, spices, oakum, wool, and hides. The sun made it worse, but the boy, I think, preferred it strong. After wandering along many old quays, and through the openings of dark sheds that, on so sunny a day, were stored with cool night and cubes and planks of gold, he found his ship, the *Mulatto Girl*. She was for the Brazils. Now it is clear that one even wiser in shipping affairs than a boy would have expected to see a craft that was haughty and portentous when bound for the Brazils, a ship that looked equal to making a coast of that kind. There she was, her flush deck well below the quay wall. A ladder went down to her, for she was no more than a schooner of a little over one hundred tons. If that did not look like the beginning of one of those voyages reputed to have ended with the Elizabethans, then I am trying to convey a wrong impression. On the deck of the *Mulatto Girl* was her master, in shirt and trousers and a remarkable straw hat more like a canopy, bending over to discharge some weighty words into the hatch. He rose and looked up at the boy on the quay, showing then a taut black beard and formidable eyes. With his hands on his hips, he surveyed for a few seconds, without speaking, the messenger above. Then he talked business, and more than legitimate business. "Do you want to come?" he asked, and smiled. "Eh?" He stroked his beard. (The Brazils and all! A ship like that!) "There's a berth for you. Come along, my son." And observe what we may lose through that habit of ours of uncritical obedience to duty; see what may leave us for ever in that fatal pause, caused by the surprise of the challenge to our narrow experience and knowledge, the pause in which we allow habit to overcome adventurous instinct! I never heard again of the *Mulatto Girl*. I could not expect to. Something, though, was gained that day. It cannot be named. It is of no value. It is, you may have guessed, that very light which it has been admitted may since have gone out.

Well, nobody who has ever surprised that light in Dockland will be persuaded that it is not there still, and will remain. But what could strangers see of it? The foreshore to them is the unending monotony of grey streets, sometimes grim, often decayed, and always reticent and sullen, that might never have seen the stars nor heard of good luck; and the light would be, when closely looked at, merely a high gas bracket on a dank wall in solitude, its glass broken, and the flame within it fluttering to extinction like an imprisoned and crippled moth trying to evade the squeeze of giant darkness and the wind. The narrow and forbidding by-path under that glim, a path intermittent and depending on the weight of the night which is trying to blot it out altogether, goes to Wapping Old Stairs. Prince Rupert once went that way. The ketch *Nonsuch*, Captain Zachary Gillam, was then lying just off, about to make the voyage which established the Hudson's Bay Company.

It is a path, like all those stairs and ways that go down to the River, which began when human footsteps first outlined London with rough tracks. It is a path by which the descendants of those primitives went out of London, when projecting the original enterprise of their forbears from Wapping to the Guinea Coast and Manitoba. Why should we believe it is different today? The sea does not change, and seamen are what they were if their ships are not those we admired many years ago in the India Docks. It is impossible for those who know them to see those moody streets of Dockland, indeterminate, for they follow the River, which run from Tooley Street by the Hole-in-the-Wall to the Deptford docks, and from Tower Hill along Wapping High Street to Limehouse and the Isle of Dogs, as strangers would see them. What could they be to strangers? Mud, taverns, pawnshops, neglected and obscure churches, and houses that might know nothing but ill-fortune.

So they are; but those ways hold more than the visible shades. The warehouses of that meandering chasm which is Wapping High Street are like weathered and unequal cliffs. It is hard to believe sunlight ever falls there. It could not get down. It is not easy to believe the River is near. It seldom shows. You think at times you hear the distant call of a ship. But what would that be? Something in the mind. It happened long ago. You, too, are a ghost left by the vanished past. There is a man above at a high loophole, the topmost cave of a warehouse which you can see has been exposed to commerce and the elements for ages; he pulls in a bale pendulous from the cable of a derrick. Below him one of the horses of a van tosses its nose-bag. There is no other movement. A carman leans against an iron post, and cuts bread and cheese with a clasp-knife. It was curious to hear that steamer call, but we knew what it was. It was from a ship that went down, we have lately heard, in the War, and her spectre reminds us, from a voyage which is over, of men we shall see no more. But the call comes again just where the Stairs, like a shining wedge of day, hold the black warehouses asunder, and give us the light of the River and a release to the outer world. And there, moving swiftly across the brightness, goes a steamer outward bound.

That was what we wanted to know. She confirms it, and her signal, to whomever it was made, carries farther than she would guess. It is understood. The past for some of us now is our only populous and habitable world, invisible to others, but alive with whispers for us. Yet the sea still moves daily along the old foreshore, and ships still come and go, and do not, like us, run aground on what now is not there.

II
A Midnight Voyage

Our voyage was to begin at midnight from near Limehouse Hole. The hour and the place have been less promising in the beginning of many a strange adventure. Where the voyage would end could not be said, except that it would be in Bugsby's Reach, and at some time or other. It was now ten o'clock, getting towards sailing time, and the way to the foreshore was unlighted and devious. Yet it was somewhere near. This area of still and empty night railed off from the glare of the Commercial Road would be Limehouse Church. It is foolish to suppose you know the Tower Hamlets because you have seen them by day. They change. They are like those uncanny folk of the fables. At night, wonderfully, they become something else, take another form, which has never been more than glimpsed, and another character, so fabulous and secret that it will support the tales of the wildest romanticist, who rightly feels that if such yarns were told of 'Frisco or Timbuctoo they might get found out. Was this the church? Three Chinamen were disputing by its gate. Perhaps they were in disagreement as to where the church would be in daylight.

At a corner where the broad main channel of electric light ended, and perplexity began, a policeman stood, and directed me into chaos. "Anywhere," he explained, "anywhere down there will do." I saw a narrow alley in the darkness, which had one gas lamp and many cobbled stones. At the bottom of the lane were three iron posts. Beyond the posts a bracket lamp showed a brick wall, and in the wall was an arch so full of gloom that it seemed impassable, except to a steady draught of cold air that might have been the midnight itself entering Limehouse from its own place. At the far end of that opening in the wall was nothing. I stood on an invisible wooden platform and looked into nothing with no belief that a voyage could begin from there. Before me then should have been the Thames, at the top of the flood tide. It was not seen. There was only a black void dividing some clusters of brilliant but remote and diminished lights. There were odd stars which detached themselves from the fixed clusters, and moved in the void, sounding the profundity of the chasm beneath them with lines of trembling fire. Such a wandering comet drifted near where I stood on the verge of nothing, and then it was plain that its trail of quivering light did not sound, but floated and undulated on a travelling road—that chasm before me was black because it was filled with fluid night. Night, I discovered suddenly, was in irresistible movement. It was swift and heavy. It was unconfined. It was welling higher to douse our feeble glims and to founder London, built of shadows on its boundary. It moved with frightful quietness. It seemed confident of its power. It swirled and eddied by the piles of the wharf, and there it found a voice, though that was muffled; yet now and then it broke into levity for a moment, as at some shrouded and alien jest.

There were sounds which reached me at last from the opposite shore, faint with distance and terror. The warning from an unseen steamer going out was as if a soul, crossing this Styx, now knew all. There is no London on the Thames, after sundown. Most of us know very little of the River by day. It might then be no more native to our capital than the Orientals who stand under the Limehouse gas lamps at night. It surprises us. We turn and look at it from our seat in a tram, and watch a barge going down on the ebb—it luckily misses the piers of Blackfriars Bridge—as if a door had unexpectedly opened on a mystery, revealing another world in London, and another sort of life than ours. It is as uncanny as if we had sensed another dimension of space. The tram gets among the buildings again, and we are reassured by the confined and arid life we know. But what a light and width had that surprising world where we saw a barge drifting as leisurely as though the narrow limits which we call reality were there unknown!

But after dark there is not only no River, when you stand where by day is its foreshore; there is no London. Then, looking out from Limehouse, you might be the only surviving memory of a city that has vanished. You might be solitary among the unsubstantial shades, for about you are only comets passing through space, and inscrutable shapes; your neighbours are Cassiopeia and the Great Bear.

But where was our barge, the *Lizzie*? I became aware abruptly of the skipper of this ship for our midnight voyage among the stars. He had his coat-collar raised. The *Lizzie*, he said, was now free of the mud, and he was going to push off. Sitting on a bollard, and pulling out his tobacco-pouch, he said he hadn't had her out before. Sorry he'd got to do it now. She was a bitch. She bucked her other man overboard three days ago. They hadn't found him yet. They found her down by Gallions Reach. Jack Jones was the other chap. Old Rarzo they called him. Took more than a little to give him that colour. But he was All Right. They were going to give a benefit concert for his wife and kids. Jack's brother was going to sing; good as Harry Lauder, he is.

Below us a swirl of water broke into mirth, instantly suppressed. We could see the *Lizzie* now. The ripples slipped round her to the tune of they-'avn't-found-'im-yet, they-'avn't-found-'im-yet-they 'avn't. The skipper and crew rose, fumbling at his feet for a rope. There did not seem to be much of the *Lizzie*. She was but a little raft to drift out on those tides which move among the stars. "Now's your chance," said her crew, and I took it, on all fours. The last remnant of London was then pushed from us with a pole. We were launched on night, which had begun its ebb towards morning.

The punt sidled away obliquely for mid-stream. I stood at one end of it. The figure of Charon could be seen at the other, of long acquaintance with this passage, using his sweep with the indifference of habitude. Perhaps it was not Charon. Yet there was some obstruction to the belief that we were bound for no more than the steamer *Aldebaran*, anchored in Bugsby's Reach. From the low deck of the barge it was surprising that the River, whose name was Night, was content with the height to which it had risen. Perhaps it was taking its time. It might soon receive an influx from space, rise then in a silent upheaval, and those low shadows that were London, even now half foundered, would at once go. This darkness was an irresponsible power. It was the same flood which had sunk Knossos and Memphis. It was tranquil, indifferent, knowing us not, reckoning us all one with the Sumerians. They were below it. It had risen above them. Now the time had come when it was laving the base of London.

The crew cried out to us that over there was the entrance to the West India Dock. We knew that place in another life. But should Charon joke with us? We saw only chaos, in which the beams from a reputed city glimmered without purpose.

The shadow of the master of our black barge pulled at his sweep with a slow confidence that was fearful amid what was sightless and unknown. His pipe glowed, as with the profanity of an immortal to whom eternity and infinity are of the usual significance. Then a red and green eye appeared astern, and there was a steady throbbing as if some monster were in pursuit of us. A tug shaped near us, drew level, and exposed with its fires, as it went ahead, a radiant *Lizzie* on an area of water that leaped in red flames. The furnace door of the tug was shut, and at once we were blind. "Hold hard," yelled our skipper, and the *Lizzie* slipped into the turmoil of the tug's wake.

There would be Millwall. The tug and the turmoil had gone. We were alone again in the beyond. There was no sound now but the water spattering under our craft, and the fumbling and infrequent splash of the sweep. Once we heard the miniature bark of a dog, distinct and fine, as though distance had refined it as well as reduced it. We were nearly round the loop the River makes about Millwall, and this unknown region before us was Blackwall Reach by day, and Execution Dock used to be dead ahead. To the east, over the waters, red light exploded fan-wise and pulsed on the clouds latent above, giving them momentary form. It was as though, from the place where it starts, the dawn had been released too soon, and was at once recalled. "The gas works," said the skipper.

Still the slow drift, quite proper to those at large in eternity. But this, I was told, was the beginning of Bugsby's Reach. It was first a premonition, then a doubt, and at last a distinct tremor in the darkness ahead of us. A light appeared, grew nearer, higher, and brighter, and there was a suspicion of imminent mass. "Watch her," warned the skipper. Watch what? There was nothing to watch but the dark and some planets far away, one of them red. The menacing one still grew higher and brighter. It came at us. A wall instantly appeared to overhang us, with a funnel and masts above it, and our skipper's yell was lost in the thunder of a churning propeller. The air shuddered, and a siren hooted in the heavens. A long, dark body seemed minutes going by us, and our skipper's insults were taken in silence by her superior deck. She left us riotous in her wake, and we continued our journey dancing our indignation on the uneasy deck of the *Lizzie*.

The silent drift recommenced, and we neared a region of unearthly lights and the smell of sulphur, where aerial skeletons, vast and black, and columns and towers, alternately glowed and vanished as the doors of infernal fires were opened and shut. We drew abreast of this phantom place where names and darkness battled amid gigantic ruin. Charon spoke. "They're the coal wharves," he said.

The lights of a steamer rose in the night below the wharves, but it was our own progress which brought them nearer. She was anchored. We made out at last her shape, but at first she did not answer our hail.

"Hullo, *Aldebaran*," once more roared our captain.

There was no answer. In a minute we should be by her, and too late.

"Barge ahoy!" came a voice. "Look out for a line."

III
A Shipping Parish

What face this shipping parish shows to a stranger I do not know. I was never a stranger to it. I should suppose it to be a face almost vacant, perhaps a little conventionally picturesque, for it is grey and seamed. It might be even an altogether expressionless mask, staring at nothing. Anyhow, there must be very little to be learned from it, for those bright young cultured strangers, admirable in their eagerness for social service, who come and live with us for a time, so that they may understand the life of the poor, never seem to have made anything of us. They say they have; they speak even with some amount of assurance, at places where the problem which is us is examined aloud by confident politicians and churchfolk. But I think they know well enough that they always failed to get anywhere near what mind we have. There is a reason for it, of course. Think of honest and sociable Mary Ann, of Pottles Rents, E., having been alarmed by the behaviour of good society, as it is betrayed in the popular picture Press, making odd calls in Belgravia (the bells for visitors, too), to bring souls to God.

My parish, to strangers, must be opaque with its indifference. It stares beyond the interested visitor, in the way the sad and disillusioned have, to things it supposes a stranger would not understand if he were told. He has reason, therefore, to say we are dull. And Dockland, with its life so uniform that it could be an amorphous mass overflowing a reef of brick cells, I think would be distressing to a sensitive stranger, and even a little terrifying, as all that is alive but inexplicable must be. No more conscious purpose shows in our existence than is seen in the coral polyp. We just go on increasing and forming more cells. Overlooking our wilderness of tiles in the rain—we get more than a fair share of rain, or else the sad quality of wet weather is more noticeable in such a place as ours—it seems a dismal affair to present for the intelligent labours of mankind for generations. Could nothing better have been done than that? What have we been busy about?

Well, what are people busy about anywhere? Human purpose here has been as blind and sporadic as it is at Westminster, unrelated to any fixed star, lucky to fill the need of the day, building without any distant design, flowing in bulk through the lowest channels that offered. As elsewhere, it is obstructed by the unrecognized mistakes of its past. Our part of London, like Kensington or Islington, is but the formless accretion of countless swarms of life which had no common endeavour; and so here we are, Time's latest deposit, the vascular stratum of this area of the earth's rind, a sensitive surface flourishing during its day on the piled strata of the dead. Yet this is the reef to which I am connected by tissue and bone. Cut the kind of life you find in Poplar and I must bleed. I cannot detach myself, and write of it. Like any other atom, I would show the local dirt, if examined. My hand moves, not loyally so much as instinctively, to impulses which come from beneath and so out of a stranger's knowledge; out of my own, too, largely.

Is that all? Not quite. Where you, if you came to us, would see but an unremarkable level of East-Enders, much like other Londoners, with no past worth recording, and no future likely to be worth a book of gold, I see, looking to the past, a spectral show of fine ships and brave affairs, and good men forgotten, or almost forgotten, and moving among the plainer shades of its foreground some ghosts well known to me. I think they were what are called failures in life. And turning from those shades, and their work which went the way of all forgotten stuff before the inexorable tide of affairs, I look forward from Poplar, unreasonably hopeful (for so we are made), though this time into the utter dark, for the morning that shall show us the more enduring towers of the city of our dreams, the heart of the commune, the radiant spires of the city that shall be lovelier than that dear city of Cecrops.

But for those whose place it is not, memories and dreams can do nothing to transform it. Dockland would seem to others as any alien town would seem to me. There is something, though, you must grant us, a heritage peculiarly ours. Amid our packed tenements, into the dark mass where poorer London huddles as my shipping parish, are set our docks. Embayed in the obscurity are those areas of captured day, reservoirs of light brimmed daily by the tides of the sun, silver mirrors through which one may leave the dark floor of Poplar for radiant other worlds. We have our ships and docks, and the River at Blackwall when night and the flood come together, and walls and roofs which topmasts and funnels surmount, suggestions of a vagabondage hidden in what seemed so arid a commonplace desert. These are of first importance. They are our ways of escape. We are not kept within a division of the map. And Orion, he strides over our roofs on bright winter nights. We have the immortals. At the most, your official map sets us only lateral bounds. The heavens here are as high as elsewhere. Our horizon is beyond our own limits. In this faithful chronicle of our parish I must tell of our boundaries as I know them. They are not so narrow as you might think. Maps cannot be so carefully planned, nor walls built high enough nor streets confined and strict enough, to hold within limits our lusty and growing population of thoughts. There is no census you can take which will give you forewarning of what is growing here, of the way we increase and expand. Take care. Some day, when we discover the time has come for it, we shall tell our numbers, and be sure you will then learn the result. Travelling through our part of the country, you see but our appearance. You go, and report us casually to your friends, and forget us. But when you feel the ground moving under your feet, that will be us.

From my high window in central Dockland, as from a watch tower, I look out over a tumbled waste of roofs and chimneys, a volcanic desert, inhabited only by sparrows and pigeons. Humanity burrows in swarms below that surface of crags, but only faint cries tell me that the rocks are caverned and inhabited, that life flows there unseen through subterranean galleries. Often, when the sunrise over the roofs is certainly the coming of Aurora, as though then the first illumination of the sky heralded the veritable dayspring for which we look, and the gods were nearly here, I have watched for that crust beneath, which seals the sleepers under, to heave and roll, to burst, and for released humanity to pour through fractures, from the lower dark, to be renewed in the fires of the morning. Nothing has happened yet. But I am confident it would repay society to appoint another watcher when I am gone, to keep an eye on the place.

Right below my window there are two ridges running in parallel jags of chimneys, with a crevasse between them to which I can see no bottom. But a roadway is there. From an acute angle of the window a cornice overhangs a sheer fall of cliff. That is as near the ground as can be got from my outlook. Several superior peaks rise out of the wilderness, where the churches are; and beyond the puzzling middle distance, where smoke dissolves all form, loom the dock warehouses, a continuous range of far dark heights. I have thoughts of a venturesome and lonely journey by moonlight, in and out of the chimney stacks, and all the way to the distant mountains. It looks inviting, and possible, by moonlight. And, indeed, any bright day in summer, from my window, Dockland with its goblin-like chimneys might be the enchanted country of a child's dream, where shapes, though inanimate, are watchful and protean. From that silent world legions of grotesques move out of the shadows at a touch of sunlight, and then, when you turn on them in surprise, become thin and vague, either phantoms or smoke, and dissolve. The freakish light shows in little what happens in the long run to man's handiwork, for it accelerates the speed of change till change is fast enough for you to watch a town grow and die. You see that Dockland is unstable, is in flux, alters in colours and form. I doubt whether the people below are sensitive to this ironic display on their roofs.

My eyes more frequently go to one place in that high country. In that distant line of warehouses is a break, and there occasionally I see the masts and spars of a tall ship, and I remember that beyond my dark horizon of warehouses is the path down which she has come from the Indies to Blackwall. I said we were not inland. Cassiopeia is in that direction, and China over there.

For my outlook is more than the centre of Dockland. I call it the centre of the world. Our high road is part of the main thoroughfare from Kensington to Valparaiso. Every wanderer must come this way at least once in his life. We are the hub whence all roads go to the circumference. A ship does not go down but we hear the cry of distress, and the house of a neighbour rocks on the flood and is lost, casting its people adrift on the blind tides.

Think of some of our street names—Malabar Street, Amoy Place, Nankin Street, Pekin Street, Canton Street. And John Company has left its marks. You pick up hints of the sea here as you pick old shells out of dunes. We have, still nourishing in a garden, John Company's Chapel of St. Matthias, a fragment of a time that was, where now the vigorous commercial life of the Company shows no evidence whatever of its previous urgent importance. Founded in the time of the Commonwealth as a symbol for the Company's men who, when in rare moments they looked up from the engrossing business of their dominant hours, desired a reminder of the ineffable things beyond ships and cargoes, the Chapel has survived all the changes which destroyed their ships and scattered the engrossing business of their working hours into dry matter for antiquaries. So little do men really change. They always leave their temples, whether they lived in Poplar or Nineveh. Only the names of their gods change. The Chapel at Poplar it was then, when this shipping parish had no docks, and the nearest church was over the fields to Stepney. Our vessels then lay in the river. We got our first dock, that of the West India Merchants, at the beginning of last century. A little later the East India Dock was built by John Company. Then another phase began to reshape Dockland. There came a time when the Americans looked in a fair way, sailing ahead fast with the wonderful clippers Donald McKay was building at Boston, to show us a tow rope. The best sailers ever launched were those Yankee ships, and the Thames building yards were working to create the ideal clipper which should beat them. This really was the last effort of sails, for steamers were on the seas, and the Americans were actually making heroic efforts to smother them with canvas. Mr. Green, of Poplar, worried over those Boston craft, declared we must be first again, and first we were. But both Boston and Poplar, in their efforts to perfect an old idea, did not see a crude but conquering notion taking form to magnify and hasten both commerce and war.

But they were worth doing, those clippers, and worth remembering. They sail clear into our day as imperishable memories. They still live, for they did far more than carry merchandise. When an old mariner speaks of the days of studding sails it is not the precious freight, the real purpose of his ships, which animates his face. What we always remember afterwards is not the thing we did, or tried to do, but the friends who were about us at the time. But our stately ships themselves, with our River their home, which gave Poplar's name, wherever they went, a ring on the counter like a sound guinea, at the most they are now but planks bearded with sea grass, lost in ocean currents, sighted only by the albatross.

Long ago nearly every home in Dockland treasured a lithographic portrait of one of the beauties, framed and hung where visitors could see it as soon as they entered the door. Each of us knew one of them, her runs and her records, the skipper and his fads, the owner and his prejudice about the last pennyworth of tar. She was not a transporter to us, an earner of freights, something to which was attached a profit and loss account and an insurance policy. She had a name. She was a sentient being, perhaps noble, perhaps wilful; she might have any quality of character, even malice. I have seen hands laid on her with affection in dock, when those who knew her were telling me of her ways.

To few of the newer homes among the later streets of Dockland is that beautiful lady's portrait known. Here and there it survives, part of the flotsam which has drifted through the years with grandmother's sandalwood chest, the last of the rush-bottomed chairs, and the lacquered tea-caddy. I well remember a room from which such survivals were saved when the household ship ran on a coffin, and foundered. It was a front parlour in one of the streets with an Oriental name; which, I cannot be expected to remember, for when last I was in that room I was lifted to sit on one of its horsehair chairs, its seat like a hedgehog, and I was cautioned to sit still. It was rather a long drop to the floor from a chair for me in those days, and though sitting still was hard, sliding part of the way would have been much worse. That was a room for holy days, too, a place for good behaviour, and boots profaned it. Its door was nearly always shut and locked, and only the chance formal visit of respect-worthy strangers brought down its key from the top shelf of the kitchen dresser. That key was seldom used for relatives, except at Christmas, or when one was dead. The room was always sombre. Light filtered into it through curtains of wire gauze, fixed in the window by mahogany frames. Over the door by which you entered was the picture of an uncle, too young and jolly for that serious position, I thought then, with his careless neckcloth, and his cap pulled down over one eye. The gilt moulding was gone from a corner of the picture—the only flaw in the prim apartment—for once that portrait fell to the floor, and on the very day, it was guessed, that his ship must have foundered.

A round table set on a central thick leg having a three-clawed foot was in that chamber, covered with a cloth on which was worked a picture from the story of Ruth. But only puzzling bits of the latter were to be seen, for on the circumference of the table-cover were books, placed at precise distances apart, and in the centre was a huge Bible, with a brass clasp. With many others my name was in the Bible, and my birthday, and a space left blank for the day of my death. Reflected in the pier-glass which doubled the room were the portraits in oils of my grandparents, looking wonderfully young, as you may have noticed is often the case in people belonging to ancient history, as though, strangely enough, people were the same in those remote days, except that they wore different clothes.

I have often sat on the chair, and when patience had inured me to the spines of the area I occupied, looked at the reflections in the mirror of those portraits, for they seemed more distant so, and in a perspective according to their age, and became really my grandparents, in a room, properly, of another world, which could be seen, but was not. A room no one could enter any more. I remember a black sofa, which smelt of dust, an antimacassar over its head. That sofa would wake to squeak tales if I stood on it to inspect the model of a ship in yellow ivory, resting on a wall-bracket above. There were many old shells in the polished brass fender, some with thick orange lips and spotted backs; others were spirals of mother-o'-pearl, which took different colours for every way you held them. You could get the only sound in the room by putting the shells to your ear. Like the people of the portraits, it was impossible to believe the shells had ever lived. The inside of the grate was filled with white paper, and the trickles of fine black dust which rested in its crevices would start and run stealthily when people walked in the next room. Over the looking-glass there hung a pair of immense buffalo horns, with a piece of curly black hair dividing them which looked like the skin of our retriever dog. Above the horns was the picture of "The Famous Tea Clipper *Oberon*, setting her Studding Sails off the Lizard"; but so high was the print, and so faint—for the picture, too, was old—that some one grown up had to tell me all about it.

The clipper *Oberon* long since sailed to the Isle-of-No-Land-at-All, and the room in which her picture hung has gone also, like old Dockland, and is now no more than something remembered. The clipper's picture went with the wreckage, when the room was strewn, and I expect in that house today there is a photograph of a steamer with two funnels.

Nothing conjures back that room so well as the recollection of a strange odour which fell from it when its door opened, as though something bodiless passed as we entered. There was never anything in the room which alone could account for the smell, for it had in it something of the sofa, which was old and black, and of the lacquered tea-caddy, within the lid of which was the faint ghost of a principle indefinably ancient and rare; and there was in it, too, something of the shells. But you could never find where the smell really came from. I have tried, and know. A recollection of that strange dusky fragrance brings back the old room on a summer afternoon, so sombre that the mahogany sideboard had its own reddish light, so quiet that the clock could be heard ticking in the next room; time, you could hear, going leisurely. There would be a long lath of sunlight, numberless atoms swimming in it, slanting from a corner of the window to brighten a patch of carpet. Two flies would be hovering under the ceiling. Sometimes they would dart at a tangent to hover in another place. I used to wonder what they lived on. You felt secure there, knowing it was old, but seeing things did not alter, as though the world were established and content, desiring no new thing. I did not know that the old house, even then, quiet and still as it seemed, was actually rocking on the flood of mutable affairs; that its navigator, sick with anxiety and bewilderment in guiding his home in the years he did not understand, which his experience had never charted, was sinking nerveless at his helm. For he heard, when his children did not, the premonition of breakers in seas having no landmark that he knew; felt the trend and push of new and inimical forces, and currents that carried him helpless, whither he would not go, but must, heartbroken, into the uproar and welter of the modern.

I have been told that London east of the Tower has no history worth mentioning, and it is true that sixteenth-century prints show the town to finish just where the Dock of St. Katherine is now. Beyond that, and only marshes show, with Stebonhithe Church and a few other signs to mark recognizable country. On the south side the marshes were very extensive, stretching from the River inland for a considerable distance. The north shore was fen also, but a little above the tides was a low eminence, a clay and gravel cliff, that sea-wall which now begins below the Albert Dock and continues round the East Anglian seaboard. Once it serpentined as far as the upper Pool, disappearing as the wharves and docks were built to accommodate London's increasing commerce. There is no doubt, then, that the Lower Thames parishes are really young; but, when we are reminded that they have no history worth mentioning, it may be understood that the historian is simply not interested enough to mention it.

So far as age goes my shipping parish cannot compare with a cathedral city; but antiquity is not the same as richness of experience. One remembers the historic and venerable tortoise. He is old enough, compared with us. But he has had nothing so varied and lively as the least of us can show. Most of his reputed three hundred years is sleep, no doubt, and the rest vegetables. In the experience of Wapping, Poplar, Rotherhithe, Limehouse, and Deptford, when they really came to life, there was precious little sleep, and no vegetables worth mentioning. They were quick and lusty. There they stood, long knee-deep and busy among their fleets, sometimes rising to cheer when a greater adventure was sailing or returning, some expedition that was off to find further avenues through the Orient or the Americas, or else a broken craft bringing back tragedy from the Arctic; ship after ship; great captain after great captain. No history worth mentioning! There are Londoners who cannot taste the salt. Yet, no doubt, it is difficult for younger London to get the ocean within its horizon. The memory of the *Oberon*, that famous ship, is significant to me, for she has gone, with all her fleet, and some say she took Poplar's best with her. Once we were a famous shipping parish. Now we are but part of the East End of London. The steamers have changed us. The tides do not rise high enough today, and our shallow waters cannot make home for the new keels.

But to the old home now the last of the sailing fleet is loyal. We have enough still to show what once was there; the soft gradations of a ship's entrance, rising into bows and bowsprit, like the form of a comber at its limit, just before it leaps forward in collapse. The mounting spars, alive and braced. The swoop and lift of the sheer, the rich and audacious colours, the strange flags and foreign names. South Sea schooner, whaling barque from Hudson's Bay, the mahogany ship from Honduras, the fine ships and barques that still load for the antipodes and 'Frisco. Every season they diminish, but some are still with us. At Tilbury, where the modern liners are, you get wall sides mounting like great hotels with tier on tier of decks, and funnels soaring high to dominate the day. There the prospect of masts is a line of derrick poles. But still in the upper docks is what will soon have gone for ever from London, a dark haze of spars and rigging, with sometimes a white sail floating in it like a cloud. We had a Russian barquentine there yesterday. I think a barquentine is the most beautiful of ships, the most aerial and graceful of rigs, the foremast with its transverse spars giving breadth and balance, and steadying the unhindered lift skywards of main and mizzen poles. The model of this Russian ship was as memorable as a Greek statue. It is a ship's sheer which gives loveliness to her model, like the waist of a lissom woman, finely poised, sure of herself, in profile. She was so slight a body, so tall and slender, but standing alert and illustriously posed, there was implied in her slenderness a rare strength and swiftness. And to her beauty of line there went a richness of colour which made our dull parish a notable place. She was of wood, painted white. Her masts were of pine, veined with amber. Her white hull, with the drenchings of the seas, had become shot with ultramarine shadows, as though tinctured with the virtue of the ocean. The verdigris of her sheathing was vivid as green light; and the languid dock water, the colour of jade, glinting round her hull, was lambent with hues not its own. You could believe there was a soft radiation from that ship's sides which fired the water about her, but faded when far from her sides, a delicate and faery light which soon expired.

Such are our distinguished visitors in Dockland, though now they come to us with less frequency. If the skipper of the *Oberon* could now look down the Dock Road from the corner by North Street, what he would look for first would be, not, I am sure, what compelled the electric trams, but for the entrance of the East Dock and its familiar tangle of spars. He would not find it. The old dock is there, but a lagoon asleep, and but few vessels sleeping with it. The quays are vacant, except for the discarded lumber of ships, sun-dried boats, rusted cables and anchors, and a pile of broken davits. The older dock of the West India Merchants is almost the same. Yet even I have seen the bowsprits and jib-booms of the Australian packets diminish down the quays of the East Dock as an arcade; and of that West Dock there is a boy who well remembers its quays buried under the largess of the tropics and the Spanish Main, where now, through the colonnades of its warehouse supports, the vistas are empty. Once you had to squeeze sideways through the stacked merchandise. There were huge hogsheads of sugar and hillocks of coconuts. Molasses and honey escaped to spread a viscid carpet which held your feet. The casual prodigality of it expanded the mind. Certainly this earth must be a big and cheerful place if it could spread its treasures thus wide and deep in a public place under the sky. It corrected the impression got from the retail shops for any penniless youngster, with that pungent odour of sugar crushed under foot, with its libations of syrup poured from the plenty of the sunny isles. Today the quays are bare and deserted, and grass rims the stones of the footway, as verdure does the neglected stone covers in a churchyard. In the dusk of a winter evening the high and silent warehouses which enclose the mirrors of water enclose too an accentuation of the dusk. The water might be evaporating in shadows. The hulls of the few ships, moored beside the walls, become absorbed in the dark. Night withdraws their substance. What the solitary wayfarer sees then is the incorporeal presentment of ships. Dockland expires. The living and sounding day is elsewhere, lighting the new things on which the young are working. Here is the past, deep in the obscurity from which time has taken the sun, where only memory can go, and sees but the ineffaceable impression of what once was there.

There is a notable building in our Dock Road, the Board of Trade offices, retired a little way from the traffic behind a screen of plane trees. Not much more than its parapet appears behind the foliage. By those offices, on fine evenings, I find one of our ancients, Captain Tom Bowline. Why he favours the road there I do not know. It would be a reasonable reason, but occult. The electric trams and motor buses annoy him. And not one of the young stokers and deck-hands just ashore and paid off, or else waiting at a likely corner for news of a ship, could possibly know the skipper and his honourable records. They do not know that once, in that office, Tom was a famous and respected figure. There he stands at times, outside the place which knew him well, but has forgotten him, wearing his immemorial reefer jacket, his notorious tall white hat and his humorous trousers—short, round, substantial columns—with a broad line of braid down each leg.

His face is weather-stained still, and though his hair is white, it has the form of its early black and abundant vitality. As long ago as 1885 he landed from his last ship, and has been with us since, watching the landmarks go. "The sea," he said to me once, "the sea has gone. When I look down this road and see it so empty—(the simple truth is it was noisy with traffic)—I feel I've overstayed my time allowance. My ships are firewood and wreckage, my owners are only funny portraits in offices that run ten-thousand-ton steamers, and the boys are bones. Poplar? This isn't Poplar. I feel like Robinson Crusoe—only I can't find a footprint in the place."

It is for the young to remember there is no decay, though change, sometimes called progress, resembles it, especially when your work is finished and you are only waiting and looking on. When Captain Tom is in that mood we go to smoke a pipe at a dockhead. It will be high tide if we are in luck, and the sun will be going down to give our River majesty, and a steamer will be backing into the stream, outward bound. The quiet of a fine evening for Tom, and the great business of ships and the sea for me. We see the steamer's captain and its pilot leaning over the bridge, looking aft towards the River. I think the size of their vessel is a little awful to Tom. He never had to guide so many thousand tons of steel and cargo into a crowded waterway. But those two young fellows above know nothing of the change; they came with it. They are under their spell, thinking their world, as once Tom did his, established and permanent. They are keeping easy pace with the movement, and so do not know of it. Tom, now at rest, sitting on a pierhead bollard, sees the world leaving him, going ahead past his cogitating tobacco smoke. Let it go. We, watching quietly from our place on the pier-head, are wiser than the moving world in one respect. We know it does not know whence it is moving, nor why. Well, perhaps its presiding god, who is determined the world shall go round, would be foolish to tell us.

The sun has dropped behind the black serration of the western city. Now the River with all the lower world loses substance, becomes vaporous and unreal. Moving so fast then? But the definite sky remains, a hard dome of glowing saffron based on thin girders of iron clouds. The heaven alone is trite and plain. The wharves, the factories, the ships, the docks, all the material evidence of hope and industry, merge into a dim spectral show in which a few lights burn, fumbling with ineffectual beams in dissolution. Out on the River a dark body moves past; it has bright eyes, and hoots dismally as it goes.

There is a hush, as though at sunset the world had really resolved, and had stopped moving. But from the waiting steamer looming over us, a gigantic and portentous bulk, a thin wisp of steam hums from a pipe, and hangs across the vessel, a white wraith. Yet the hum of the steam is too subdued a sound in the palpable and oppressive dusk to be significant. Then a boatswain's pipe rends the heavy dark like the gleam of a sword, and a great voice, awed by nothing, roars from the steamer's bridge. There is a sudden commotion, we hear the voice again, and answering cries, and by us, towards the black chasm of the River in which hover groups of moving planets, the mass of the steamer glides, its pale funnel mounting over us like a column. Out she goes, turning broadside on, a shadow sprinkled with stars, then makes slow way down stream, a travelling constellation occulting one after another all the fixed lights.

Captain Tom knocks out his pipe on the heel of his boot, his eyes still on the lights of the steamer. "Well," says Tom, "they can still do it. They don't want any help old Tom could give aboard her. A good man there. Where's she bound for, I wonder?"

Now who could tell him that? What a question to ask me. Did Tom ever know his real destination? Not he! And have I not watched Dockland itself in movement under the sun, easily mobile, from my window in its midst? Whither was it bound? Why should the old master mariner expect the young to answer that? He is a lucky navigator who always finds his sky quite clear, and can set his course by the signs of unclouded heavenly bodies, and so is sure of the port to which his steering will take him.

IV
The Heart's Desire

If the evening was one of those which seem longer than usual but still have far to go, it was once a custom in Millwall to find a pair of boots of which it could be claimed that it was time they were mended, and to carry the artful parcel around to Mr. Pascoe. His cobbler's shop was in a street that had the look of having retired from the hurry and press of London, aged, dispirited, and indifferent even to its defeat, and of waiting vacantly for what must come to elderly and shabby despondence. Each grey house in the street was distinguished but by its number and the ornament which showed between the muslin curtains of its parlour window. The home of the Jones's had a geranium, and so was different from one neighbour with a ship's model in gypsum, and from the other whose sign was a faded photograph askew in its frame. On warm evenings some of the women would be sitting on their doorsteps, watching with dull faces their children at play, as if experience had told them more than they wanted to know, but that they had nothing to say about it. Beyond this street there was emptiness. It ended, literally, on a blind wall. It was easy for a wayfarer to feel in that street that its life was caught. It was secluded from the main stream, and its children were a lively yet merely revolving eddy. They could not get out. When I first visited Mr. Pascoe, as there was no window ornament to distinguish his place from the others, and his number was missing, I made a mistake, and went next door. Through a hole drilled in that wrong door a length of cord was pendant, with a greasy knot at its end. Underneath the knot was chalked "Pull." I pulled. The door opened on a mass of enclosed night. From the street it was hard to see what was there, so I went inside. What was there might have been a cavern—narrow, obscure, and dangerous with dim obstructions. Some of the shadows were darker than others, because the cave ended, far-off, on a port-light, a small square of day framed in black. Empty space was luminous beyond that cave. Becoming used to the gloom I saw chains and cordage hanging from the unseen roof. What was faintly like the prow of a boat shaped near. Then out from the lumber and suggestions of things a gnome approached me. "Y' want ole Pascoe? Nex' dore, guv'nor!" At that moment, in the square of bright day at the end of the darkness, the apparition of a ship silently appeared, and was gone again before my surprise. That open space beyond was London River.

Next door, in a small room to which day and night were the same, Mr. Pascoe was always to be found bending over his hobbing foot, under a tiny yellow fan of gaslight which could be heard making a tenuous shrilling whenever the bootmaker looked up, and ceased riveting. When his head was bent over his task only the crown of a red and matured cricketing cap, which nodded in time to his hammer, was presented to you. When he paused to speak, and glanced up, he showed a face that the gas jet, with the aid of many secluded years, had tinctured with its own artificial hue, a face puckered through a long frowning intent on old boots. He wore an apron that had ragged gaps in it. He was a frail and dingy little man, and might never have had a mother, but could have been born of that dusty workroom, to which he had been a faithful son all his life. It was a murky interior shut in from the day, a litter of petty tools and nameless rubbish on a ruinous bench, a disorder of dilapidated boots, that mean gas jet, a smell of leather; and there old Pascoe's hammer defiantly and rapidly attacked its circumstances, driving home at times, and all unseen, more than those rivets. If he rose to rake over his bench for material or a tool, he went spryly, aided by a stick, but at every step his body heeled over because one leg was shorter than the other. Having found what he wanted he would wheel round, with a strange agility that was apparently a consequence of his deformity, continuing his discourse, and driving his points into the air with his hammer, and so hobble back, still talking; still talking through his funny cap, as his neighbours used to say of him. At times he convoluted aerial designs and free ideas with his hammer, spending it aloft on matters superior to boots. The boots were never noticed. Pascoe could revivify his dust. The glitter of his spectacles when he looked up might have been the sparkling of an ardent vitality suppressed in his little body.

The wall space of his room was stratified with shelves, where half-seen bottles and nondescript lumps were to be guessed at, like fossils embedded in shadow. They had never been moved, and they never would be. Hanging from a nail on one shelf was a framed lithograph of the ship *Euterpe*, off S. Catherine's Point, July 21, 1849. On the shelf below the picture was a row of books. I never saw Pascoe look at them, and they could have been like the bottles, retained by a careful man because of the notion that some day they would come in handy. Once, when waiting for Pascoe, who was out getting a little beer, I glanced at the volumes, and supposed they bore some relation to the picture of the ship; perhaps once they had been owned by that legendary brother of Pascoe's, a sailor, of whom I had had a misty apprehension. It would be difficult to say there had been a direct word about him. There were manuals on navigation, seamanship, and ship-building, all of them curiosities, in these later days, rather than expert guides. They were full of marginal notes, and were not so dusty as I had expected to find them. The rest of the books were of journeys in Central America and Mexico: *Three Years in Guatemala*; *The Buried Cities of Yucatan*; *Scenes on the Mosquito Coast*; *A Voyage to Honduras*. There was more of it, and of that sort. They were by authors long forgotten; but those books, too, looked as though they were often in use. Certainly they could not be classed with the old glue-pots and the lumber.

It was long after my first visit to Pascoe that he referred to those books. "Somebody told me," he said one evening, while offering me a share of his beer, "that you have been to the American tropics."

I told him I could say I had been, but little more. I said it was a very big world.

"Yes," he said, after a pause: "and what a world. Think of those buried cities in Yucatan—lost in the forest, temples and gods and everything. Men and women there, once upon a time, thinking they were a fine people, the only great people, with a king and princesses and priests who made out they knew the mysteries, and what God was up to. And there were processions of girls with fruit and flowers on feast-days, and soldiers in gold armour. All gone, even their big notions. Their god hasn't got even a name now. Have you ever read the *Companions of Columbus*?"

I was as surprised as though one of his dim bottles in the shadows had suddenly glowed before my eyes, become magical with moving opalescence. What right had old Pascoe to be staring like that to the land and romance of the Toltecs? I had been under the impression that he read nothing but the Bible and *Progress and Poverty*. There was a biography of Bradlaugh, too, which he would quote copiously, and his spectacles used fairly to scintillate over that, and his yellow face to acquire a new set of cunning and ironic puckers; for I believe he thought, when he quoted Bradlaugh—whose name was nearly all I knew of that famous man—that he was becoming extremely modern, and a little too strong for my conventional and sensitive mind. But here he was, telling of Incas, Aztecs, and Toltecs, of buried cities, of forgotten treasures, though mainly of the mind, of Montezuma, of the quetzal bird, and of the vanished splendour of nations that are now but a few weathered stones. It was the forlorn stones, lost in an uninhabited wilderness, to which he constantly returned. A brother of his, who had been there, perhaps had dropped a word once into Pascoe's ear while his accustomed weapon was uplifted over a dock-labourer's boot-heel, and this was what that word had done. Pascoe, with a sort of symbolic gesture, rose from his bobbing foot before me, tore the shoe from it, flung it contemptuously on the floor, and approached me with a flamboyant hammer.

And that evening I feared for a moment that Pascoe was spoiled for me. He had admitted me to a close view of some secret treasured charms of his memory, and believing that I was not uninterested, now, of course, he would be always displaying, for the ease of his soul, supposing we had a fellowship and a bond, his fascinating quetzals and Toltecs. Yet I never heard any more about them. There was another subject though, quite homely, seeing where we both lived, and equally absorbing for us both. He knew our local history, as far as our ships and house-flags were concerned, from John Company's fleet to the *Macquarie*. He knew, by reputation, many of our contemporary master mariners. He knew, and how he had learned it was as great a wonder as though he spoke Chinese, a fair measure of naval architecture. He could discuss ships' models as some men would Greek drama. He would enter into the comparative merits of rig suitable for small cruising craft with a particularity which, now and then, gave me a feeling almost akin to alarm; because in a man of Pascoe's years this fond insistence on the best furniture for one's own little ship went beyond fair interest, and became the day-dreaming of romantic and rebellious youth. At that point he was beyond my depth. I had forgotten long ago, though but half Pascoe's age, what my ship was to be like, when I got her at last. Knowing she would never be seen at her moorings, I had, in a manner of speaking, posted her as a missing ship.

One day I met at his door the barge-builder into whose cavernous loft I had stumbled on my first visit to Pascoe. He said it was a fine afternoon. He invited me in to inspect a figure-head he had purchased. "How's the old 'un?" he asked, jerking a thumb towards the bootmaker's. Then, with some amused winking and crafty tilting of his chin, he signed to me to follow him along his loft. He led me clean through the port-light of his cave, and down a length of steps outside to his yard on the foreshore of the Thames, where, among his barges hauled up for repairs, he paused by a formless shape covered by tarpaulins.

"I've seen a few things in the way of boats, but this 'ere's a—well, what do you make of it?" He pulled the tarpaulin back, and disclosed a vessel whose hull was nearing completion. I did not ask if it was Pascoe's work. It was such an amusing and pathetic surprise, that, with the barge-builder's leering face turned to me waiting for my guess, there was no need to answer. "He reckons," said the barge-builder, "that he can do a bit of cruising about the mouth of the Thames in that. 'Bout all she wants now is to have a mast fitted, and to keep the water out, and she'll do." He chuckled grimly. Her lines were crude, and she had been built up, you could see, as Pascoe came across timber that was anywhere near being possible. Her strakes were a patchwork of various kinds of wood, though when she was tarred their diversity would be hidden from all but the searching of the elements. It was astonishing that Pascoe had done so well. It was still more astonishing that he should think it would serve.

"I've given him a hand with it," remarked the barge-builder, "an' more advice than the old 'un 'ud take. But I dessay 'e could potter about with the dam' tub round about as far as Canvey, if 'e keeps it out of the wash of the steamers. He's been at this job two years now, and I shan't be sorry to see my yard shut of it. . . . Must humour the old boy, though. . . . Nigglin' job, mending boots, I reckon. If I mended boots, I'd 'ave to let orf steam summow. Or go on the booze."

I felt hurt that Pascoe had not taken me into his confidence, and that his ship, so far as I was concerned, did not exist. One Saturday evening, when I called, his room was in darkness. Striking a match, there was his apron shrouding his hobbing foot. This had never happened before, and I turned into the barge-builder's. The proprietor there faced me silently for a moment, treasuring a jest he was going to give me when I was sufficiently impatient for it. "Come to see whether your boots are done? Well, they ain't. Pascoe's gone. Christened his boat this morning, and pushed off. Gone for a trial trip. Gone down river."

"Good Lord," I said, or something of the sort.

"Yes," continued the barge-builder, luxuriating in it, "and I've often wondered what name he'd give her, and he done it this morning, in gold leaf. D'yer remember what she looked like? All right. Well, 'er name is the *Heart's Desire*, and her skipper will be back soon, if she don't fall apart too far off."

Her skipper was not back soon, nor that day. We had no news of him the next day. A few women were in his workshop, when I called, hunting about for footwear that should have been repaired and returned, but was not. "'Ere they are," cried one. "'Ere's young Bill's boots, and nothing done to 'em. The silly old fool. Why didn't 'e tell me 'e was going to sea? 'Ow's young Bill to go to school on Monday now?" The others found their boots, all urgently wanted, and all as they were when Pascoe got them. A commination began of light-minded cripples who took in young and innocent boots, promising them all things, and then treacherously abandoned them, to do God knew what; and so I left.

This became serious; for old Pascoe, with his *Heart's Desire*, had vanished, like his Toltecs. A week went by. The barge-builder, for whom this had now ceased to be a joke, was vastly troubled by the complete disappearance of his neighbour, and shook his head over it. Then a few lines in an evening paper, from a port on the Devon coast, looked promising, though what they wished to convey was not quite clear, for it was a humorous paragraph. But the evidence was strong enough for me, and on behalf of the barge-builder and a few others I went at once to that west-coast harbour.

It was late at night when I arrived, and bewildering with rain, total darkness, and an upheaval of cobbles in by-ways that wandered to no known purpose. But a guide presently brought me to a providential window, and quarters in the *Turk's Head*. In my room I could hear a continuous murmuring, no doubt from the saloon bar below, and occasional rounds of hearty merriment. That would be the place for news, and I went down to get it. An oil-lamp veiled in tobacco smoke was hanging from a beam of a sooty ceiling. A congregation of longshoremen, visible in the blue mist and smoky light chiefly because of their pink masks, was packed on benches round the walls. They laughed aloud again as I went in. They were regarding with indulgent interest and a little shy respect an elegant figure overlooking them, and posed negligently against the bar, on the other side of which rested the large bust of a laughing barmaid. She was as amused as the men. The figure turned to me as I entered, and stopped its discourse at once. It ran a hand over its white brow and curly hair with a gesture of mock despair. "Why, here comes another to share our *Hearts Desire*. We can't keep the beauty to ourselves."

It was young Hopkins, known to every reader of the *Morning Despatch* for his volatility and omniscience. It was certainly not his business to allow any place to keep its secrets to itself; indeed, his reputation including even a capacity for humour, the world was frequently delighted with more than the place itself knew even in secret. Other correspondents from London were also in the room. I saw them vaguely when Hopkins indicated their positions with a few graceful flourishes of his hand. They were lost in Hopkins's assurance of occupying superiority. They were looking on. "We all got here yesterday," explained Hopkins. "It's a fine story, not without its funny touches. And it has come jolly handy in a dull season when people want cheering up. We have found the Ancient Mariner. He was off voyaging again but his ship's magic was washed out by heavy weather. And while beer is more plentiful than news, we hope to keep London going with some wonders of the deep."

In the morning, before the correspondents had begun on the next instalment of their serial story, I saw Pascoe sitting up in a bed at another inn, his expenses an investment of the newspaper men. He was unsubdued. He was even exalted. He did not think it strange to see me there, though it was not difficult to guess that he had his doubts about the quality of the publicity he had attracted, and of the motive for the ardent attentions of his new and strange acquaintances from London. "Don't be hard on me," he begged, "for not telling you more in London. But you're so cautious and distrustful. I was going to tell you, but was uncertain what you'd say. Now I've started and you can't stop me. I've met a man here named Hopkins, who has given me some help and advice. As soon as my craft is repaired, I'm off again. It was unlucky to meet that sou'wester in July. But once out of home waters, I ought to be able to pick up the Portuguese trade wind off Finisterre, and then I'm good for the Caribbees. I'll do it. She should take no more than a fortnight to put right."

There was no need to argue with him. The *Heart's Desire*, a centre of attraction in the place, answered any doubt I had as to Pascoe's safety. But he was humoured. Hopkins humoured him, even openly encouraged him. The Heart's Desire was destined for a great adventure. The world was kept in anticipation of the second departure for this strange voyage to Guatemala. The *Heart's Desire* on the edge of a ship-repairer's yard, was tinkered, patched, refitted, made as right as she could be. The ship-repairer, the money for the work made certain for him, did what he was told, but made no comment, except to interrogate me curiously when I was about.

A spring tide, with a southerly wind, brought us to a natural conclusion. An unexpected lift of the water washed off the *Heart's Desire*, rolled her about, and left her broken on the mud. I met the journalists in a group on their way to the afternoon train, their faces still reflecting the brightness of an excellent entertainment. Hopkins took me aside. "I've made it right with old Pascoe. He hasn't lost anything by it, you can be sure of that." But I was looking for the cobbler, and all I wished to learn was the place where I was likely to find him. They did not know that.

Late that evening I was still looking for him, and it had been raining for hours. The streets of the village were dark and deserted. Passing one of the many inns, which were the only illumination of the village, I stumbled over a shadow on the cobbles outside. In the glow of a match I found Pascoe, drunk, with his necessary stick beside him, broken.

V
The Master

This master of a ship I remember first as a slim lad, with a shy smile, and large hands that were lonely beyond his outgrown reefer jacket. His cap was always too small for him, and the soiled frontal badge of his line became a coloured button beyond his forelock. He used to come home occasionally — and it was always when we were on the point of forgetting him altogether. He came with a huge bolster in a cab, as though out of the past and nowhere. There is a tradition, a book tradition, that the boy apprenticed to the sea acquires saucy eyes, and a self-reliance always ready to dare to that bleak extreme the very thought of which horrifies those who are lawful and cautious. They know better who live where the ships are. He used to bring his young shipmates to see us, and they were like himself. Their eyes were downcast. They showed no self-reliance. Their shyness and politeness, when the occasion was quite simple, were absurdly incommensurate even with modesty. Their sisters, not nearly so polite, used to mock them.

As our own shy lad was never with us for long, his departure being as abrupt and unannounced as his appearance, we could willingly endure him. But he was extraneous to the household. He had the impeding nature of a new and superfluous piece of furniture which is in the way, yet never knows it, and placidly stays where it is, in its wooden manner, till it is placed elsewhere. There was a morning when, as he was leaving the house, during one of his brief visits to his home, I noticed to my astonishment that he had grown taller than myself. How had that happened? And where? I had followed him to the door that morning because, looking down at his cap which he was nervously handling, he had told me he was going then to an examination. About a week later he announced, in a casual way, that he had got his masters ticket. After the first shock of surprise, caused by the fact that this information was an unexpected warning of our advance in years, we were amused, and we congratulated him. Naturally he had got his certificate as master mariner. Why not? Nearly all the mates we knew got it, sooner or later. That was bound to come. But very soon after that he gave us a genuine surprise, and made us anxious. He informed us, as casually, that he had been appointed master to a ship; a very different matter from merely possessing the licence to command.

We were even alarmed. This was serious. He could not do it. He was not the man to make a command for anything. A fellow who, not so long ago, used to walk a mile with a telegram because he had not the strength of character to face the lady clerk in the post office round the corner, was hardly the man to overawe a crowd of hard characters gathered by chance from Tower Hill, socialize them, and direct them successfully in subduing the conflicting elements of a difficult enterprise. Not he. But we said nothing to discourage him.

Of course, he was a delightful fellow. He often amused us, and he did not always know why. He was frank, he was gentle, but that large vacancy, the sea, where he had spent most of his young life, had made him—well, slow. You know what I mean. He was curiously innocent of those dangers of great cities which are nothing to us because we know they are there. Yet he was always on the alert for thieves and parasites. I think he enjoyed his belief in their crafty omnipresence ashore. Proud of his alert and knowing intelligence, he would relate a long story of the way he had not only frustrated an artful shark, but had enjoyed the process in perfect safety. That we, who rarely went out of London, never had such adventures, did not strike him as worth a thought or two. He never paused in his merriment to consider the strange fact that to him, alone of our household, such wayside adventures fell. With a shrewd air he would inform us that he was about to put the savings of a voyage into an advertised trap which a country parson would have stepped over without a second contemptuous glance,

He took his ship away. The affair was not discussed at home, though each of us gave it some private despondency. We followed him silently, apprehensively, through the reports in the *Shipping Gazette*. He made point after point safely—St. Vincent, Gibraltar, Suez, Aden—after him we went across to Colombo, Singapore, and at length we learned that he was safe at Batavia. He had got that steamer out all right. He got her home again, too. After his first adventure as master he made voyage after voyage with no more excitement in them than you would find in Sunday walks in a suburb. It was plain luck; or else navigation and seamanship were greatly overrated arts.

A day came when he invited me to go with him part of his voyage. I could leave the ship at Bordeaux. I went. You must remember that we had never seen his ship. And there he was, walking with me to the dock from a Welsh railway station, a man in a cheap mackintosh, with an umbrella I will not describe, and he was carrying a brown paper parcel. He was appropriately crowned with a bowler hat several sizes too small for him. Glancing up at his profile, I actually wondered whether the turmoil was now going on in his mind over that confession which now he was bound to make; that he was not the master of a ship, and never had been.

There she was, a bulky modern freighter, full of derricks and time-saving appliances, and her funnel lording it over the neighbourhood. The man with the parcel under his arm led me up the gangway. I was not yet convinced. I was, indeed, less sure than ever that he could be the master of this huge community of engines and men. He did not accord with it.

We were no sooner on deck than a man in uniform, grey-haired, with a seamed and resolute face, which any one would have recognized at once as a sailor's, approached us. He was introduced as the chief officer. He had a tale of woe: trouble with the dockmaster, with the stevedores, with the cargo, with many things. He did not appear to know what to do with them. He was asking this boy of ours.

The skipper began to speak. At that moment I was gazing at the funnel, trying to decipher a monogram upon it; but I heard a new voice, rapid and incisive, sure of its subject, resolving doubts, and making the crooked straight. It was the man with the brown paper parcel. That was still under his arm—in fact, the parcel contained pink pyjamas, and there was hardly enough paper. The respect of the mate was not lessened by this.

The skipper went to gaze down a hatchway. He walked to the other side of the ship, and inspected something there. Conned her length, called up in a friendly but authoritative way to an engineer standing by an amid-ship rail above. He came back to the mate, and with an easy precision directed his will on others, through his deputy, up to the time of sailing. He beckoned to me, who also, apparently, was under his august orders, and turned, as though perfectly aware that in this place I should follow him meekly, in full obedience.

Our steamer moved out at midnight, in a drive of wind and rain. There were bewildering and unrelated lights about us. Peremptory challenges were shouted to us from nowhere. Sirens blared out of dark voids. And there was the skipper on the bridge, the lad who caused us amusement at home, with this confusion in the dark about him, and an immense insentient mass moving with him at his will; and he had his hands in his pockets, and turned to tell me what a cold night it was. The pier-head searchlight showed his face, alert, serene, with his brows knitted in a little frown, and his underlip projecting as the sign of the pride of those who look direct into the eyes of an opponent, and care not at all. In my berth that night I searched for a moral for this narrative, but went to sleep before I found it.

VI
The Ship-Runners

1

The *Negro Boy* tavern is known by few people in its own parish, for it is a house with nothing about it to distinguish its fame to those who do not know that a man may say to his friend, when their ships go different ways out of Callao, "I may meet you at the *Negro Boy* some day." It is in a road which returns to the same point, or near to it, after a fatiguing circuit of the Isle of Dogs. No part of the road is better than the rest. It is merely a long road. That day when I first heard of Bill Purdy I was going to the tavern hoping to meet Macandrew, Chief of the *Medea*. His ship was in again. But there was nobody about. There was nothing in sight but the walls, old, sad, and discreet, of the yards where ships are repaired. The dock warehouses opposite the tavern offered me their high backs in a severer and apparently an endless obduracy. The *Negro Boy*, as usual, was lost and forlorn, but resigned to its seclusion from the London that lives, having stood there long enough to learn that nothing can control the ways of changing custom. Its windows were modest and prim in green curtains. Its only adornment was the picture, above its principal door, of what once was a negro boy. This picture now was weathered into a faded plum-coloured suit and a pair of silver shoe-buckles—there was nothing left of the boy himself but the whites of his eyes. The tavern is placed where men moving in the new ways of a busy and adventurous world would not see it, for they would not be there. Its dog Ching was asleep on the mat of the portico to the saloon bar; a Chinese animal, in colour and mane resembling a lion whose dignity has become sullenness through diminution. He could doze there all day, and never scare away a chance customer. None would come. But men who had learned to find him there through continuing to trade to the opposite dock, would address him with some familiar and insulting words, and stride over him.

The tavern is near one of the wicket gates of the irregular intrusion into the city of a maze of dock basins, a gate giving those who know the district a short cut home from the ships and quays; the tavern was sited not altogether without design. And there came Macandrew through that gate, just as I had decided I must try again soon. His second, Hanson, was with him. They crossed to the public-house, and we stooped over the yellow lump of Chinese apathy to talk to him, and went through the swing doors into the saloon. The saloon was excluded from the gaze of the rest of the house by little swinging screens of frosted glass above the bar, for that was where old friends of the landlord met, who had known him all the time their house-flags had been at home in the neighbouring docks; and perhaps had even sailed with him when be himself went to sea. A settee in red plush, salvage from the smoke-room of a liner, ran round the walls, with the very mahogany tables before it which it knew when afloat. Some men in dingy uniforms and dungarees were at the tables. Two men I did not know stood leaning over the bar talking confidentially across it to a woman who was only a laugh, for she was hidden. One of the men turned from the counter to see who had come in.

"Hullo Mac," he cried, in a voice hearty with the abandon of one who, perhaps, had been there long enough; "look here, here's Jessie says she's going to leave us."

A woman's hand, spoiled by many heavy rings, moved across the counter and shook his arm in warning. The youngster merely closed his own hand over it. "Isn't it hard. Really going to forsake us. Won't mix your whiskey or uncork my lemonade any more. What are we going to do when we come home now?"

There was an impatient muttering beyond him, and he made public a soothing and exaggerated apology. All the men in the room, even the group bent over a diagram of a marine engine they had drawn in chalk on their table, looked up in surprise, first at the youngster who had raised his voice, and then to watch the tall shadow of a woman pass quickly down the counter-screen and vanish. Still laughing, the young man, with his uniform cap worn a little too carelessly, nodded to the company, and went out with his companion.

Macandrew stared in contempt at the back of the fellow as he went. "A nice boy that. Too bright and bonny for my ship. What's that he was saying about Jessie?" He tried to see where she was, and lowered his voice. "I know his kind. I saw them together last night, in the Dock Road. What does she have anything to do with him for? We know her of course . . . but even then. . . . She's really not a bad sort. She's like that with all those young dogs. Can't help it, I suppose."

He moved to the bar, a massive figure, beyond the age of a sea-going engineer, but still as light on his feet as a girl. "Where's she gone?" He pushed open one of the little glass screens, and put his petulant face, with its pale eyes set like aquamarines in bronze, into an opening too small to frame it. "Can you see her, Hanson?"

Hanson winked at me, adjusted the spectacles on his nose, and grinned. With that grin, and his spectacles, he was as surprising as a handsome gargoyle. His height compelled him to lean forward and to grin downward, even when speaking to a big man like Macandrew. He turned to his chief now, and both hands went up to his spectacles. In the way the corners of his mouth turned up before he spoke, whimsically wrinkling his nose, and in his intent and amused regard, there was a suggestion of the mockery of a low immortal for beings who are fated earnestly to frustrate themselves. His grin gave you the uncomfortable feeling that it was useless to pretend you were keeping nothing from him.

"Here goes," said Hanson. "Never mind Jessie. I've got something to tell you, Chief. I'm leaving you this voyage."

Macandrew was instantly annoyed. "Going? Dammit, you can't. Look at the crowd I've got now. You mustn't do it."

"I must. They are a thin lot, but you could push the old *Medea* along with anything. I've got another ship. My reason is very good, from the way I look at it."

Hanson turned his grin to me. He was going to enjoy the privilege of seeing his reasons deemed unreasonable. "Don't think it's a better job I've got. It's worse. It's a very rummy voyage. We may complete it, with luck. It's a boat-running lunacy, and some mining gear. She's called the *Cygnet*. I've been over her, and we shall call her something different before we see the last of her."

"Then why are you going?" I asked him.

"To see what will happen. . . ."

Macandrew interrupted him. "What? And you next on the list for Chief? You're romantic, young man, and that means you're no engineer. Is there a lot of money in it?"

"There isn't, but there's some life. I want to know what I'm made of. Shall I ever learn it under you? Down below in the *Medea* is like winding up a clock and going to sleep. Do you know the *Cygnet* has six inches of freeboard?" He was talking to me, but kept glancing sideways to see what effect this had on Macandrew. But Macandrew's broad back was impassive.

"Six inches of freeboard, barring her false bulwarks of deal boards, and she's going out to—I forget the name of the place, but I could show you where it is within a hundred miles on a map that doesn't give its name. It's up the Pondurucu."

Macandrew made no sign, and Hanson, his humour a little damped, spoke more seriously. "I don't think she'll ever get there, but it will be interesting to see where she stops, and why."

Macandrew heaved round on his junior. "There's drivel. It sounds well from an engineer and a mathematician, doesn't it?" He turned away again. "Supposing," he said, over his shoulder, "supposing you pull this ship through all right, then where will you be? Any better off?"

"I think so," said Hanson. He couldn't talk to Macandrew's back, so he bent over me and pointed a challenging finger at my necktie. "I've never risked anything yet, not even my job. This is where I do it. It'll be nice to attempt something when the odds are that you can't finish it, and there's nothing much in it if you do. Why," he said, grinning at his Chief's back, "if I were to stay with him I'd become so normal that I'd slip into marriage and safety as a matter of course, and have to give up everything."

"Who's in charge of this lunacy?" asked Macandrew. His voice was a little truculent.

"All right, Chief. I shan't remember his name any the better because you're annoyed with me. I haven't seen the skipper yet. I think I heard him called Purdy."

"Purdy? Bill Purdy?" Macandrew was incredulous. "Do you know what you've let yourself in for? If Purdy's got the job, I know why. Nobody else would take it, and he's the last man, anyway, who ought to have it."

"What, drink?" asked Hanson.

"Lord, no. Not Purdy. No. It's the man himself. I've known him a long time, and I like him, but he'll never do. He can't make up his mind to a course. Don't you remember the *Campeachy* case? I expect it was before your time. Purdy had her. He was coming up-Channel, and got nervous over the weather, and put into Portland for a pilot. There was no pilot. So he decided to put out again and go on. It never occurred to him that as he was in shelter he'd better stay there till a pilot arrived, because getting out of that was exactly when he'd want one. He put her ashore. That was like Purdy, to play for safety and make a wreck. When he got over the fuss Lloyd's raised about it he refused to take command again for some time. He couldn't even make up his mind whether he wanted a ship at all."

Hanson listened to this with the air of one who was being reassured in a doubtful enterprise.

"You mistake me, Chief," he said. "You are only improving my reasons for going. Not only is the ship crank, but so is her skipper. Now tell me . . ."

Macandrew frowned at his junior, and his curiously pale eyes became distinctly inhuman. I believe he thought his counsel was being laughed at. But the door opened, and he touched Hanson's arm. A little man of middle age stood there, who turned, and actually prevented the doors from swinging together with their usual announcement of another customer. For only a moment he raised his downcast eyes to see who was there, and then nodded sadly to Macandrew. His drooping moustache conformed to the downward lines of his face, which was that of a man who had been long observing life with understanding, and had not a lively opinion of it.

Macandrew's demeanour changed. It was now mild and almost affectionate as he greeted the little man. "Come over here, Purdy, and tell us what you've been doing. Here's Hanson, this young fellow. I hear he's sailing with you. He's your Chief. You'd better know him."

Purdy raised his eyes in a grave and momentary survey, made to shake hands with Hanson, but hesitated, and did so only because Hanson put out his own great fist with decision. Purdy did not speak, except to say to Hanson: "We're signing-on tomorrow. I'll meet you at the shipping office then." He seemed to forget the pair of them, paused, and went to a far vacant corner of the bar. The barmaid, as he got there, returned, and stopped to say something to him.

"Well, I'm damned," muttered Macandrew. "Look here, Jessie," he cried, "here's all us young men been waiting for nearly twenty minutes, and you take no notice of us, but as soon as a captain looks across the counter, there you are. But how did you know he was a captain? That's what I'd like to know. He's only wearing a bowler hat."

2

The *Medea* had been ordered unexpectedly to Barry for loading, to take the place of an unready sister-ship; and Macandrew, of whom I have had much experience, would be active, critical of what a dog must put up with in life, and altogether unfit for intimate, amiable, and reminiscent conversation. Yet I wanted to see him again before he left, and went past the Board of Trade Office hoping for signs of the *Medea*, for I had heard she was assembling a crew that morning. But the marine-store shops, with their tarpaulin suits hanging outside open-armed and oscillating, looked across to the men lounging against the shipping-office railings, and the idlers stared across at the tarpaulins. It did not appear to be a place where anything was destined to happen. It merely looked like rain.

Macandrew might be inside with his crowd of firemen and greasers. Behind the brass grille there a clerk, solitary and absorbed in his duties, bent over a pile of ships' articles, and presented to the seamen in the public space beyond him only the featureless shine of a bald head. The seamen, scattered about in groups, shabby and listless, with a few of their officers among them, were as sombre and subdued as though they had learned life had nothing more to offer them, and they were present only because they might as well use up the salvage of their days. The clerk raised his head and questioned the men before him with a quick, inclusive glance. "Any men here of the *Cygnet*?" he demanded. His voice, raised in certainty above the casual murmuring of the repressed, made them all as self-conscious and furtive as though discovered in guilt. Hanson's head appeared above the crowd, as he rose from a bench and went to the official. "I'm the engineer of the *Cygnet*. We're waiting for Captain Purdy."

The clerk complained. He pulled out his watch. "He said he would be ready for me at ten this morning. Now you've lost your turn, and there are three other ships." He turned away in a manner which told every one that Hanson had now become non-existent, pushed aside the *Cygnet's* papers, and searched the room once more. "Ah, good morning, Captain Hudson. You ready for me? Then I'll take you next." The captain went around to stand beside the official, and his crew clustered on their side of the bars, with their caps in their hands.

"A good start that," said Hanson to me. "Perhaps, after all, we never shall start. Must be a rum chap, that Purdy."

He told me the *Medea's* crowd was there, but perhaps Macandrew had already signed, and so would not appear. That meant I might not see him for another year; but as I left the office I found him coming up its steps outside, and not as though there were the affairs of a month to be got into two days, but in leisurely abstraction. He might have been making up his mind that, after all, there was no need to call there, for he was studying each step as if he were looking for the bottom of a mystery. His fingers were twirling the little ivory pig he carries as a charm on his watchguard. The pig is supposed to assist him when he is in a difficulty. He raised his eyes.

"Anyhow," he despaired to me with irrelevance, "I can't do anything for him."

I waited for the chance of a clue. "I thought," Macandrew quietly soliloquized, "he knew better than that. He's been a failure, but all the same, he's got a better head than most of us. She's sure to bring him to grief."

"What's all this about?" I ventured.

"I've just been talking to Purdy. You remember what Hanson said of that voyage he's making? Purdy is taking Jessie with him. You don't know Purdy, but I do. And I know Jessie; but that's nothing."

"Taking her with him?" I asked; "but how. . . ."

"Oh, cook, of course. That'll be it. She'll be steward, naturally. That's reasonable. You've seen her. Jessie's the sort of woman would jump at the chance of such a pleasant trip, as cook."

"I don't understand. . . ."

"Who said you did? Nobody does but the pair of them. I know what another man might see in Purdy. But a woman! He's middle-aged, quiet, and looks tired. That woman is young and lively, and she'll be bored to death with him on such a trip."

"But I thought you said . . ."

"What have I said? I've said nothing. Jessie's away to sea as cook. Why not? I'm going inside. Are you coming in?"

Crossing the floor of the office, Hanson caught Macandrew's arm. "Your lot are signing-on now." The master of the *Medea* was round with the official tallying the men by the ship's papers. "I see it," Macandrew answered. "I've signed. I wanted to catch the old man before he began that job."

"We're hung up for Purdy," Hanson told him. "Nobody seems to know where he is." Hanson was amused.

"Yes. Well . . . he'll be here all right . . . and now this new job which you think so funny, young Hanson. See it goes through. Presently it won't be so funny. Hang on to it then."

Hanson was surprised by this, and a trifle hurt. He was beginning to speak, making the usual preliminary adjustment of his spectacles, when a movement near the door checked him. His hands remained at his glasses, as if aiding his sight to certify the unbelievable.

"What's this?" he murmured. "Here's Purdy. Isn't that the *Negro Boy's* barmaid with him . . . is she with him?" He continued to watch, apparently for some sign that this coincidence of his captain and a barmaid in a public office was designed.

The bent gaze of the master of the *Cygnet* might have noticed the boots of his engineer, for he took in the room no higher than that. Then he came forward with his umbrella, still in contemplation. It might have been no more than a coincidence. She, too, approached, a little behind him, but obscuring his dull meagreness, for she was a head taller, and a bold and challenging figure. Her blond hair distinguished her even more than the emphasis of her florid hat. Her pallor that morning refined the indubious coarseness of her face, and changed vulgarity into the attractive originality of a spirited character. Many there knew her, but she recognized nobody. She yawned once, in a fair piece of acting, and in her movements and the poise of her head there was a disdain almost plain enough to be insolence. Purdy turned to her, and the strange pair conferred. I heard Hanson say to himself: "What on earth." She left Purdy, bent her head with a gracious but stressed smile to Macandrew, and went to the bench by the wall, where she sat, waiting, with her legs crossed in a way that was a defiance and an attraction in such a place, where a woman is rarely seen. She read a newspaper, perhaps because that acted as a screen, though she turned its pages with a nervous abruptness which betrayed her imitation of indifference.

3

The *Medea* and the *Cygnet*, and the other ships I knew which carried those whose fortunes were some concern of mine, might have sailed over the edge of the world. My only communication was with an occasional familiar name in the reports of the *Shipping List*. Then Macandrew came home again. But it was difficult to meet him. Mrs. Macandrew told me he was working by his ship in drydock. They had had trouble with the engines that voyage, and she herself had seen little of him, except to find him, when she came down of a morning, asleep in the drawing-room. Just flung himself down in the first place, you know. In those greasy overalls, too. He had told her the engine-room looked like a scrap-heap, but the ship had to be ready for sea in ten days. Once he had worked thirty-two hours on end. Think of that, and he had not been home for six months. She would strongly advise any girl not to marry a man who went to sea, and if I met Macandrew I was to bring him home at once. Did I hear?

When I found the *Medea* it was late in the day, for she was not in the dry-dock that had been named. Her Chief had just gone ashore. There was a chance that he would have called at the *Negro Boy*, but he had not been seen there. Except for the landlord, who was at a table talking to a stranger, the saloon was empty. A silk hat was on the table before the stranger, beside a tankard, and the hat was surmounted by a pair of neatly folded kid gloves. "Come over here," said the landlord. "Sit here for a bit, Macandrew may come in. This is Dr. Maslin." A monocle fell its length of black cord from the doctor's eye, and he nodded to me.

"The doctor used to be with me when I was running out East," explained the landlord. "Where did you say you had come from now, Doctor? Oh, yes, Tabacol. Funny name. I was never on the South American coast. After I left you sick at Macassar, the last trip we had together—the old *Siwalik*—I left the sea to younger men. But there you are, Doctor. Still at it. Why don't you give it up?"

The doctor did not answer, except to make a bubbling noise in his tankard. He placed it on the table again delicately and deliberately, and wiped his grizzled moustache with a crimson silk handkerchief. He put up his monocle, and seemed to be intently inspecting a gas globe over the counter. I thought his grimace in this concentration came from an effort to reinforce his will against all curiosity on our part. But it appeared he was really looking at what showed, at an angle, of a portrait on the wall of an inner room. He could just see it, from where he sat. Anyhow, the landlord imagined it was the portrait which had caught his friend's interest. "Looking at that crayon portrait, Doctor? Ah, showy woman, isn't she? Used to be barmaid here. The Lord knows where she is now. Went to sea, like a fool. Stewardess, or something worse. Much more useful here."

The doctor's seamed face, sour and ironic, made it impossible to know whether his expression was one of undisguised boredom, or only his show of conventional politeness. I began to feel I had broken into the intimacy of two men whose minds were dissimilar, but friendly through old associations, and that the doctor's finer wit was reproving me for an intrusion. So I rose, and asked indifferently what sort of a place was Tabacol. Had he been there before?

"Never," said the doctor, "nor is it the kind of place one wishes to see twice. We were kept at Tabacol because so many of our men were down with fever. It is a little distance up the Pondurucu River . . . maybe two hundred miles. Did you say. . . ? No. It is not really out of the way. An ocean steamer calls at Tabacol once a month or six weeks. It is only on the edge of what romantic people call the unknown."

It was evident he thought I could be one of the romantic. He looked at me for the first time, twisting the cord of his eyeglass with his finger and thumb in a fastidious way, and I thought his glance was to dissipate some doubt he had that he ought to be speaking to me at all. He dropped the cord suddenly as if letting go his reserve, and said slyly, with a grave smile: "Perhaps the romantic think the unknown is worth looking into because it may be better than what they know. At Tabacol I used to think the unknown country beyond it looked even duller than usual. There was a forest, a river, a silence, and it was either day or night. That was all. If the voice of Nature is the voice of God. . . ."

The landlord was observing in surprise this conversational excursion by his old friend, as if it were altogether new to him. He laughed aloud, and, putting a consoling hand on his friend's shoulder as he rose, he told us he must leave us for a few minutes, for he had business. "Look more cheerful before I get back, Doctor."

The doctor chuckled, and stretched across to give his gloves a more satisfactory position on his hat. "I don't understand what it can be that attracts people to such a place. Young men, maybe yourself even, wish to go there. Isn't that so? Yes. I've met such men in such places. Then they did not give me the impression that they were satisfied with their romance. Impossible, of course. Romance is never in the place unless we put it there, and who would put even a sentimental dream into such a hole as Tabacol? Tropical squalor. Broken people! I've never seen romance in such a place, and don't expect to. . . ."

Several cabs, on their way to a ship outward bound, made an increasing noise in the night, rattled by on the cobbles outside, their occupants roaring a sentimental chorus, and drowned what the doctor was saying.

". . . folly. Worse than folly." He was holding his gloves now, and was lightly flicking the edge of the table with them in place of verbal emphasis. He suddenly regarded me again as if he strongly suspected me of being his antipathy. "Who but a fool would take a woman to such a country as that? Any romantic sentimentalist, I suppose. I forget the name of the ship. There was, you might say, hardly sufficient room to paint a name on her. She was no more than a tug. It was a miracle she survived to get there at all, for she had crossed from England. Crossed the Western ocean in such a craft, and brought a woman with him. Did ever you hear of such folly?"

Now I was certain of our whereabouts, and felt a weak inclination to show an elder that I, too, knew something about it; but when I leaned forward eagerly and was about to speak, the doctor screwed in that devastating monocle, and I felt I was only a curious example of the sort of thing he especially disliked. For a minute, in which I wondered if I had quite stopped his guarded flow, he said no more. Then he addressed his eyeglass to a panel of the partition, and flicked his gloves at that.

"I had noticed for some days that little craft lying near us, but gave her no attention. I had sixteen men to attend to with complexions like lemons, and one died. There was no time to bother with other folk's troubles. Our skipper, one breakfast-time, told me there was a woman aboard that little thing, and he'd been asked whether I'd go over. She was ill.

"I've seen some queer packets of misery at sea, but never one that touched that ship. Her skipper seemed a regular fool. I had to ask him to speak up, for he mumbled like a boy who has been caught out, and knows it is useless to pretend. I learned from him that he was only just beginning his voyage. You understand? He was just beginning it, there. He was going up-river, to a point not on the chart. I cannot make out now whether he wanted to put that woman ashore to get home in comfort at the first opportunity, or whether . . . it's impossible to say. One would sooner believe the best of another man, with half a chance. After all," said the doctor bitterly, "as long as the woman survived I suppose she was some consolation in misery.

"I scrambled over the deck lumber. There was hardly room to move. I found her in a cabin where she could get little seclusion from the crew. Hardly any privacy at all, I should say. As soon as I saw her I could make a guess . . . however, I told the fellow afterwards what I thought, and he gave me no answer. He even turned his back on me. He must have known well enough that that river was no place for any sort of white woman. He was condemning her perhaps to death just to make an ugly job more attractive.

"I admit," said the doctor, with a sly glance, "that she could make it attractive, for a sort of man. She was wrapped in a rosy dressing-gown. She held it together with her hands. I noticed them . . . anybody might . . . they were covered with rings. She had character, too. She made me feel, the way she looked at me, that I was indiscreet in asking personal questions. I could see what was wrong with her. It was debility, but all the same the beginning of an end not far off, in that country.

"'You'll have to get out of this,' I told her.

"'Can't be done, Doctor,' she said coolly.

"'It can. A liner for England will be here in another week, and you must take it.'

"'I don't,' she said. She was quiet enough, but she seemed a very wilful woman. 'I've got my job here.'

"I told her that the skipper of her ship would never carry out his orders, because they could not be carried out. I told her, what was perfectly true, that their craft would rot on a sandbar, or find cataracts, or that they'd all get eaten by cannibals, or die of something nasty. I admit I tried to frighten her.

"'It's no good, Doctor,' she said. 'You can't worry me. I've got my work to do in this ship, like the others.'

"'Pooh!' I said to her. 'Cooking and that. Anybody could do it. Let the men do it. It's not a woman's job.'

"'You're wrong,' she said. 'It's mine. You don't know.'

"I began to get annoyed with this stubborn creature. I told her she would die, if she didn't leave the working of that ship to those who ought to do it.

"'Who ought?' she asked me, in a bit of a temper. 'I know what I have to do. I'm going through with it. It's no good talking. I'll take my chance, like the rest.'

"So I had to tell her that I was there because the master of her ship had sent for me to give my advice. My business was to say what she ought to do.

"'I don't want to be told. I know,' she said. 'The captain sent for you. Talk to him.'

"My temper was going, and I told her that it was something to know the captain himself had enough sense to send for me.

"'Look here,' she told me. 'I've had enough of this. I want to be alone. Thank you for troubling to come over.'"

The doctor lifted his shoulders, and made a wry face, that might have been disdain or pity.

"I was leaving her, but she called to me, and I went back. She held out her hand. 'I do thank you for troubling about me. Of course I do. But I want to stay on here—I must.'

"'Well, you know the penalty,' I said. 'I was bound to tell you that.'

"'What of it?' she said, and laughed at me. 'We musn't bother about penalties. Good-bye!'

"I must say she made me feel that if the skipper of that ship had been of different metal, she might almost have pulled him through. But what a man. What a man! I saw his miserable little figure standing not far from where my boat was when I was going. He made as if he were coming to me, and then stopped. I was going to take no notice of him, but went up and explained a thing or two. I'll bet he'll remember them. All he said was: 'I was afraid you'd never change her mind,' and turned away. What a man! There was a pair for you. I could understand him, but what could have been in her mind? Whatever made her talk like that? That's the way of it. There's your romance of the tropics, and your squalid Garden of Eden, when you know it. A monotonous and dreary job, and a woman."

The landlord returned. The monocle fixedly and significantly regarded me. "Have another, Doctor," said the landlord, pointing to the empty tankard. "How long were you in Macassar?" The doctor turned briskly to his old friend, and began some chaff.

4

Ferguson, who had just come into port with a damaged propeller shaft, was telling us how it was. This was his first expansive experience, and there could be no doubt the engine-room staff of the *Torrington* had behaved very well. The underwriters had recognized that, and handsomely, at a special meeting at Cornhill. Though Ferguson was young for a chief engineer, his professional elders, who were listening to him, showed some critical appreciation of the way he solved his problem. He was sitting at a table of the *Negro Boy*, drawing a diagram on it, and they stood round.

"There. That was where it was. You see what we had to do. It would not have been so bad in calm weather, but we were labouring heavily, all the way from Savannah. Our old man did not think it possible to do it. But it was no good waiting for something worse to happen."

The matter grew too technical for me. There was cargo jettisoned, and ballast tanks emptied aft. The stern of the *Torrington* was lifted so that her propeller at intervals was clear. Ferguson then went overside on life-lines. When he was not submerged, he was trying to put his ship right again; and when he became exhausted, one of his colleagues took his place, to see whether, while escaping drowning, he could continue the work of salvation. They all escaped, and the *Torrington* put back to Tampa for repairs, which her own engineers accomplished.

The demonstration was over, and Ferguson's story was lapsing into general gossip. The party of men began to dissolve.

"Who do you think I saw at Tampa?" Ferguson asked Macandrew. "Old Purdy."

"What?" cried Macandrew. "Is he alive?"

Ferguson laughed. "Just about. What's he been doing? I thought he had chucked the sea. It was in the Customs Office. I'd been there to make a declaration, and in one of those long corridors there he stood, all alone, with his hat in his hand, perhaps cooling his head. I hardly knew him. He's more miserable than ever."

"Did he say anything?" asked Macandrew.

"About as much as usual. I didn't know him at first. He seemed rather ill. The temples of that high forehead of his were knotted with veins. It nearly gave me a headache to look at him."

Several of us were impelled to ask a number of questions, but Ferguson was listening now, with the detachment of youth, to the end of a bawdy story that two men were laughing over. This had already displaced Purdy in his mind.

"Didn't he say anything at all? Didn't he mention Hanson?" we asked Ferguson.

"Eh? What, old Purdy? I don't think so. I don't remember. Now you mention it, I think I did hear somewhere that Hanson was with Purdy. But I don't believe he said anything about him. I was just going to ask him to come and have a drink, when he said good-bye. All I know is I saw him standing there like a sorrowful saint. Then he walked off slowly down the corridor. He's a sociable beggar. I couldn't help laughing at him."

5

There was a notice in the window of the *Negro Boy*, and I discovered that the tavern was under Entirely New Management. The picture sign over the principal door had been renewed. The mythical little figure which had given the public-house its name was no longer lost in the soot of half a century. He was now an obvious negro boy, resplendent in a golden coat. The reticence of the green window-curtains had become a bright vacancy of mirrors, and the tavern was modern within. Reform had destroyed the exclusiveness of the saloon bar; instead of privacy, distant mirrors astonished you with glimpses of your own head which were incredible and embarrassing in their novelty. The table-tops were of white marble supported on gilded iron. The prints and lithographs of ships had gone from the walls, and were replaced by real pictures converted to the advertisement of various whiskies—pictures of battleships, bull-dogs, Scotsmen, and figures in armour tempted from their ancient posts in baronial halls, after midnight, to finish the precious drink forgotten by the guests. In accordance with this transformation the young lady in attendance at the bar was in neat black and white, with her hair as compact and precise as a resolution at a public meeting which had been passed even by the women present. She was severe and decisive, and without recognition of anything there but the tariff of the house, and sold her refreshments as in a simple yet exacting ritual which she despised, but knew to be righteous.

It was many months since I had been there. Macandrew was no nearer than Rotterdam, and perhaps would not see London that voyage. There had been a long period in which change had been at work at the docks, even to their improvement, but through it all not one of my old friends had returned home. They had approached no nearer than Falmouth, the Hartlepools, or Antwerp, with a slender chance that they would come to the Thames, and next we heard of them when they were bound outwards once more, and for a period known not even to their wives. The new *Negro Boy* had not the appearance of a place where I could expect to find a friend, and I was leaving it again, instantly, when a tall figure rose in a corner waving a reassuring hand. I did not recognize the man, but thought I knew his smile, which made me look at him in dawning hope. The grin, evidently knowing its power, was maintained till I saw it indubitably as Hanson's. He made a remembered gesture with his spectacles. "I was just about sick of this place," he said. "I've waited here for an hour hoping somebody would turn up. Where's Macandrew now?"

"In Rotterdam. I don't think he will be home this voyage."

"And what's happened to this house? Where's the old man?"

"You know all I know about it. I haven't been here for nearly a year. We must expect progress to make things better than they were. Where have you come from?"

"I'm running between Liverpool and Baltimore now, in the Planets. They're comfortable ships, but I don't admire the Western ocean. It's too savage and cold. How is Macandrew? I came up from Liverpool because I felt I must see him again. I heard he was here."

From the way he talked, I thought he preferred those subjects requiring the least effort for a casual occasion. "Now and then," I had to tell him, "some of us have wondered what happened to the *Cygnet*."

Hanson's smile became effulgent. My remark might have reminded him of a most enjoyable joke, but he made no sign, while enjoying it privately, that he intended to share it with me at any time.

"There was a *Cygnet*, wasn't there?" he asked, when my patience had nearly gone. "I should like somebody to confirm it. The reason I came to this house tonight, to be candid, was just to see this room again, to settle a doubt I had. Didn't Macandrew stand over there, and show concern because a fair, plump woman wasn't quick enough with his beer?"

I admitted this, as an encouragement. "But when I got here tonight," continued Hanson, "the change made me feel my mind had lost hold. I must say it's a relief to see you."

"Has this anything to do with the *Cygnet*?" I asked.

"Everything. I had the time of my life. I wouldn't have missed it for anything. But somehow, now and then, I want to be quite sure I had it myself, and not some other fellow." He beamed with the very remembrance of the experience, and nodded his head at me. He leaned over the table to me in confidence. "Have you ever been to the tropics? I don't mean calling at Colombo or Rio. I mean the back of things where there's a remarkable sun experimenting with low life and hardly anybody looking on. If ever you get the chance, you take it. It alters all your ideas of time and space. You begin to learn what stuff life is made of when you see a tropical forest, and see nothing else for months. On the other hand," he said, "you become nothing.

You see it doesn't matter to others what happens to you, and you don't care much what happens to others."

"You don't care? It doesn't matter?" I said in doubt to this young mathematician and philosopher, who had been experimenting with life. "Isn't that merely romantic?"

"Romance—romance be damned! I got down to the facts."

"Well, get me down to them. I should like the facts. I want to hear what this strange voyage was like."

"As you know," Hanson assured me, "I went out merely to see what would happen to myself, in certain circumstances. I knew I was going to be scared, and I was. There is a place called Tabacol on the river, and we anchored there after our ocean passage for more than a week. I don't know why, and it was no use asking Purdy. Probably he didn't know. I had made up my mind to make the engines move and stop, whenever ordered, and then see where we are. Anyway, after the racket of the sea voyage, when the engines stopped at Tabacol the utter silence was as if something which had been waiting there for you at once pounced. The quiet was of an awful weight. I could hardly breathe, and chanced to look at the thermometer. It stood at 132 degrees. I don't know how I got outside, but when I came to I was on my back on deck, and Jessie was looking after me. I remember wondering then how a big, fleshy woman like her could stand it, and felt almost as sorry for her as I did for myself."

"Did she look ill?"

"Jessie? Oh, I don't know. She looked as if she might have been having a merrier time. Well, we left Tabacol, and I felt we were leaving everything we knew behind us. I got the idea, in the first day on the river, that we were quite lost, and were only pushing the old *Cygnet* along to keep up our spirits. We crawled close under the walls of the forest. Our vessel looked about as large and important as a leaf adrift. That place is so immense that I saw we were going to make no impression on it. It wouldn't matter to anybody but ourselves if it swallowed us up. On the first day I saw a round head and two yellow eyes in it, watching us go by. The thought went through my mind: 'a jaguar.' The watching face vanished on the instant, and I always felt afterwards that the forest knew all about us, but wouldn't let us know anything. I got the idea that it wasn't of the least use going on, unless we didn't intend to treat the job seriously. If we were serious about it then it was evident we ought to turn back."

"Didn't the skipper ever say what he thought of it?"

"What could Purdy think, or do? There was that river, and the forest on both sides of it, and the sun over us. Nothing else but the quiet; and we didn't know where our destination was. We anchored every evening, close to the bank. One evening, as we anchored, a shower of arrows clattered about us. There was just one shower, out of the trees, or out of the clouds."

"What was Jessie doing all this time?" I ventured to ask him.

"Why, what was any one doing? She wasn't an anxiety of my department. I suppose she was there for the only reason I had—because she asked for it. It was the same next day, except that instead of more arrows we found a python in the bunkers. Came aboard over the hawsers, I suppose. We were a lively lunatic asylum below while killing it with fire-shovels and crowbars. That was what the voyage was like. The whole lot of it was the same, and you knew quite well that the farther you went the less anything mattered. There were slight variations each day of snakes, mosquitoes, and fevers, to keep you from feeling dead already."

"I've often wondered," I confessed, thinking to bring Hanson to something I wanted to hear, "what happened to your company. Once we had a word of Purdy, but never of Jessie or of you."

"Well, now I'm telling you. But you'd have been past wondering if you'd been with us. Purdy wasn't companionable. He'd tell me it was hot. And it was. You could feel that yourself. Jessie cooked our meals. Her galley could have been only a shade better than the engine-room. She began to look rather faded. At last I was the only one who hadn't been down with fever. We crawled on and on, and the only question was where we ourselves would end, for the forest and the river were never going to. But you didn't care. I'd never been better in my life, and here was the thing I'd always wanted to see. I could have gone on for ever like that, wondering what we should see round the next corner.

"Our big troubles were to come. Up to then, we hadn't run into anything really drastic after turning a corner. I suppose we had had about a month of it, and God knows where we were, but we had nobody to ask; and then we ran on a sandbar. The jungle met overhead. We were in what was only a dark drain through the forest. So this, I thought, is where we throw in our hand. We might as well have been in another planet for all the chance we had of getting away from that place. We were aground for two days; the river then rose a foot, and we came off. The men were complaining among themselves by then. I heard them talking to each other about chucking it. It was bound to come. This day they went aft in a body to Purdy. There stood

Purdy, a little object in white against the gloom of the forest, and he looked about as futile as the last match in a wind at night. He stood fingering a beard he had grown. One of the men was beginning to talk truculently at him. Just then Jessie appeared from below, between me and the group. She had been down with fever for some days, and she surprised me as much as a ghost. She looked rather like one, too. She stood watching Purdy, without moving. He didn't look at her, though he must have known she was there. I'm pretty sure we had to thank her for what happened to us afterwards, for it was then that Purdy began shaking his finger at that big stoker who was shouting. I'd never seen him with such an expression before. As near as he could be wild, he was. 'We're going on,' said Purdy to them very distinctly. 'This ship continues her voyage. If you want to leave her here, I'll put you ashore.' He walked away some paces, and came back to the men. Then he said something more in his usual voice. 'Do you men tell me you're afraid of the job? I don't believe it. It can be done. We'll do it. We'll do it. Mr. Hanson,' he called out, 'we are ready to get under way. Would you please stand by?'

"The men never said another word. They went for'ard. It was very curious, but after that they behaved as though they had another skipper. Yet they were properly frightened by what they thought was ahead of them. My lot below were always asking me about it, and I handed them the usual ornamental and soothing lies, in which they believed long enough to keep the steam up. What more could you ask of human nature? So we kept her plugging along, getting nearer and nearer nowhere. We turned another of those dramatic corners, later on, though I forget how much later, and ahead of us the river was piled high with rocks, and was tumbling from above. The *Cygnet* had had her fair share of luck, but luck could not get her over that. We were all looking at the white water ahead, and feeling—at least I was—that we were being laughed at, when I heard Purdy call me, and turned round. He was hurrying towards me round the gear, and I thought from the look of him that this complete frustration had turned his mind. He signed for me to follow him, and I did it, wondering what we should do with a lunatic added to all the rest of it. I followed him into his cabin. 'What can I do?' he said, and bent over his berth, 'what can I do?'

"Jessie was curled up on her side in his berth, and there was nothing anyone could do. I didn't know she was alive. But she half opened her eyes, without looking up, and her hand began moving towards Purdy. 'That you, Bill?' she said. Purdy flopped down beside her. I got out.

"So I took over for a bit—the mate was no good—and waited for the next thing. That affair disheartened the men a lot, and I took it for granted, from their faces as they stood round that figure in a tarpaulin under a tree in the forest, that we were witnessing the end. There was Purdy, too . . . you couldn't expect much from him after a funeral."

Hanson bent over the table, and began tapping it with a finger, and spoke slowly through a surprise he still felt. "Old Purdy came to me the following morning, and told me what he intended to do. What do you think? He reckoned that, though we were still a hundred miles from the headquarters of the consignees, an outpost was probably no farther than just above the falls. He himself was going to prospect, for there should be a native trail through the woods, past the rapids; and he left me in charge.

"Macandrew was all wrong about that fellow. In two days he was back. He had found an outpost, four miles above, but nobody was there, so we could get no help. He was going to land our cargo of a ton and a half of machinery, and place it on the company's territory above the falls. 'You can see for yourself,' Purdy said to me pathetically, 'that I can't deliver the *Cygnet* there. But I think I am right in making her secure and leaving her here, and reporting it. What else can I do? They ought to give me a clean receipt.'

"It was funny enough, that anxiety about a ship and machinery where there was nothing but monkeys and parrots, but I agreed with him, and we got to work landing those packages of mining gear, which only an expert could understand, in a place where nothing was likely to happen till the Last Day. The way we sweated over it! And then warped the stuff with snatch blocks through four miles of jungle. Yes; and buried two men of our company on the way. But we did get the cargo on to the company's damned land at last, and a nice lot of half-naked scarecrows we looked, with nothing to fill our hollow cheeks but whiskers. There the name of the place was all right, 'Tres Irmaos,' painted over a shed. The shed was falling to pieces. There was nobody about. Nothing but a little open space, and the forest around, and the sun blazing down at us.

"We pushed on for headquarters, Purdy leading us. A hundred miles to go! I don't know how we did it. Three more died, including the mate, but we didn't bury those. Purdy kept on the move. He told me, after an eternity, that it was just ahead of us, and at last we did come to some other men. They were Colombians. We astonished them, but nothing could astonish us any more. Purdy learned that he had got to our ultimate destination all right. Then some fellow appeared, in a gaudy uniform and a sword, who spoke English. When Purdy asked to be taken to the manager of the company, this gay chap laughed fiercely, and kept looking at Purdy in triumph. 'Him?' he shouted, when he had got enough fun out of it, ''im? He's dead. We execute him. All those people—they go. No more company. All finish. No good.' He was very bright about it.

"Purdy never said a word. All he did was to turn to me, and then stare beyond me with big eyes at something which couldn't possibly have been there."

VII
Not in the Almanac

It was an unlucky Friday morning; "and, what's more," the chief officer stopped on the gangway to call down to me on the quay, "a black cat crossed my path when I left home this morning, and a very nice black cat it was." The gangway was hauled up. The tugs began to move the big steamer away from us, a process so slow that the daylight between us and the ship increased imperceptibly.

On my way home I paused by the shop which sells such antiques as old spring mattresses, china dogs, portable baths, dumb-bells, and even the kind of bedroom furniture which one would never have supposed was purchasable at second-hand. But lower, much lower in the shopkeeper's estimate than even such commodities—thrown into a bin because they were rubbish, and yet not quite valueless—was a mass of odd volumes. *The First Principles of Algebra*, *Acts Relating to Pawnbrokers*, and *Jessica's First Prayer*, were discovered in that order. The next was *Superstitions of the Sea.*

I am not superstitious. I have never met a man who was. And look at the ships in dock today, without figure-heads, with masts that are only the support of derricks and the aerials of wireless, and with science and an official certificate of competency even in the galley! Could anything happen in such ships to bring one to awe and wonder? The dark of the human mind is now lighted, one may say, with electricity. We have no shadows to make us hesitate. That book of sea superstitions was on my table, some weeks later, and a sailor, who gave up trading to the East to patrol mine-fields for three years, and who has never been known to lose any time when in doubt through wasting it on a secret propitiatory gesture, picked up the book, smiling a little superciliously, lost his smile when examining it, and then asked if he might borrow it.

We are not superstitious, now we are sure a matter may be mysterious only when we have not had the leisure to test it in the right way, but we have our private reservations. There is a ship's doctor, who has been called a hard case by those who know him, for he has grown grey and serious in watching humanity from the Guinea Coast to the South Seas. He only smiles now when listening to a religious or a political discussion, and might not be supposed to have any more regard for the mysteries than you would find in the *Cold Storage Gazette*. When he is home again we go to the British Museum. He always takes me there. It is one of his weaknesses. I invited him, when last we were there, to let us search out a certain exhibit from Egypt about which curious stories are whispered. "No you don't," he exclaimed peremptorily. He gave me no argument, but I gathered that it is very well to be funny about such coincidences, yet that one never certainly knows, and that it is better to regard the unexplored dark with a well-simulated respect till one can see through it. He had, he said, known of affairs in the East, and they were not provided for in the books; he had tried to see through them from all points, but not with the satisfaction he desired. For that reason he never invited trouble unless he knew it was not there.

Another man, very like him, a master mariner, and one who knew me well enough for secrets, was bringing me from the French Coast for Barry at full speed, in a fog. He was a clever, but an indiscreet navigator. I was mildly rebuking him by the door of his chart-room for his foolhardiness, but he laughed quietly, said he intended to make a good passage, which his owners expected, and that when the problem was straightforward he used science, but that when it was all a fog he trusted mainly to his instinct, or whatever it might be, to inform him in time. I was not to be alarmed. We should have the Lizard eight miles on the starboard beam in another hour and a half. By this time we were continuing our talk in the chart-room. An old cap of his was on the floor, upside down. I faced him there, in rebuke of this reliance on instinct, but he was staring at the cap, a little startled. Then he dashed past me without a word for the bridge. While following him at leisure I heard the telegraph ring. Outside I could see nothing but the pallor of a blind world. The flat sea was but the fugitive lustre of what might have been water; but all melted into nothing at a distance which could have been anywhere. The tremor of the ship lessened, and the noise of the wash fell, for the speed had slackened. We might have become hushed, and were waiting, listening and anxious, for something that was invisible, but threatening. Then I heard the skippers voice, quick but quiet, and arrived on the bridge in time to see the man at the wheel putting it hard over. Something had been sighted ahead of us, and now was growing broad on the starboard bow—a faint presentment of land, high and unrelated, for there was a luminous void below it. It was a filmy and coloured ghost in the sky, with a thin shine upon it of a sun we could not see. It grew more material as we watched it, and brighter, a near and indubitable coast. "I know where I am now," said the skipper. "Another minute or two, and we should have been on the Manacles."

Smiling a little awkwardly, he explained that he had seen that old cap on the floor before, without knowing how it could have got there, and at the same time he had felt very nervous, without knowing why. The last time was when, homeward bound in charge of a fine steamer, he hoped Finisterre was distant, but not too far off. Just about *there*, as it were; and that his dead reckoning was correct. The weather had been dirty, the seas heavy, and the sun invisible. He went on, to find nothing but worse weather. He did sight, however, two other steamers, on the same course as himself, evidently having calculated to pass Ushant in the morning; his own calculation. He would be off Ushant later, for his speed was less than theirs. There they were, a lucky and unexpected confirmation of his own reasoning. His chief officer, an elderly man full of doubt, smiled again, and smacked his hands together. That was all right. My friend then went into the chart-room, and underwent the strange experience we know. He wondered a little, concluded it was just as well to be on the safe side, and slightly altered his course. Early next morning he sighted Ushant. There was nothing to spare. He was, indeed, cutting it fine. The seas were great, and piled up on the rocks of that bad coast were the two steamers he had sighted the day before.

Why had not the other two masters received the same nudge from Providence before it was too late? That is what the unfortunate, who cannot genuinely offer solemn thanks like the lucky, will never know, though they continually ask. It is the darkest and most unedifying part of the mystery. Moreover, that side of the question, as a war has helped us to remember, never troubles the lucky ones. Yet I wish to add that later, my friend, when in waters not well known, in charge of a ship on her maiden voyage—for he always got the last and best ship from his owners, they having recognized that his stars were well-assorted—was warned that to attempt a certain passage, in some peculiar circumstances, was what a wise man would not lightly undertake. But my friend was young, daring, clever, and fortunate. That morning his cap was *not* on the floor. At night his valuable ship with her exceptionally valuable cargo was fast for ever on a coral reef.

What did that prove? Apart from the fact that if the young reject the experience of their elders they may regret it, just as they may regret if they do pay heed to it, his later misfortune proves nothing; except, perhaps, that the last thing on which a man should rely, unless he must, is the supposed favour of the gods of whom he knows nothing but, say, a cap unreasonably on the floor; yet gods, nevertheless, whose existence even the wise and dubious cannot flatly deny.

It may have been for a reason of such a sort that I did not lend my book to my young sailor friend who wished to borrow it. I should never have had it back. Men go to sea, and forget us. Our world has narrowed and has shut out Vanderdecken for ever. But now that everything private and personal about us which is below the notice even of the Freudian professor is pigeon-holed by officials at the Town Hall, I enjoy reading the abundant evidence for the Extra Hand, that one of the ship's company who cannot be counted in the watch, but is felt to be there. And now that every Pacific dot is a concession to some registered syndicate of money-makers, the Isle-of-No-Land-At-All, which some lucky mariners profess to have sighted, is our last chance of refuge. We cannot let even the thought of it go.

VIII
The Illusion

When I came to the house in Malabar Street to which John Williams, master mariner, had retired from the sea, his wife was at her front gate. It was evening, and from the distant River a steamer called. Mrs. Williams did not see me, for her grey head was turned away. She was watching, a little down the street, an officer of the Merchant Service, with his cap set like a challenge, for he was very young, and a demure girl with a market-basket who was with him. They were standing in amused perplexity before their house door. It was a house that had been empty since the foundering of the *Drummond Castle*. The sailor was searching his pockets for the door-key, and the girl was laughing at his pretended lively nervousness in not finding it. Mrs. Williams had not heard me stop at her elbow, and continued to watch the comedy. She had no children, and she loved young people.

I did not speak, but waited for her to turn, with that ship's call still sounding in my mind. The rain had cleared for a winter sunset. Opposite, in the house which had been turned into a frugal shop, it was thought so near to night that they lit their lamp, though it was not only possible to see the bottles of sweet-stuff and the bundles of wood in the window, but to make out the large print of a bill stuck to a pane announcing a concert at the Wesleyan Mission Room. The lamp was alight also in the little beerhouse next door to it, where the *Shipping Gazette* could be borrowed, if it were not already out on loan; for children constantly go there for it, with a request from mother, learning their geography that way in Malabar Street, while following a father or a brother round the world and back again, and working out by dead-reckoning whether he would be home for Christmas.

The quiet street, with every house alike, had that air of conscious reserve which is given by the respectable and monotonous; but for a moment then it was bright with the glory of the sky's afterglow reflected on its wet pavements, as though briefly exalted with an unexpected revelation. The radiance died. Night came, and it was as if the twilight native to the street clouded from its walls and brimmed it with gloom, while yet the sky was bright. The lamplighter set his beacon at the end of the street.

That key had been found. Mrs. Williams laughed to herself, and then saw me. "Oh," she exclaimed. "I didn't know you were there. Did you see that? That lamplighter! When Williams was at sea, and I was alone, it was quite hopeful when the lamplighter did that. It looked like a star. And that Number Ten is let at last. Did you see the young people there? I'm sure they're newly married. He's a sailor."

With the fire, the humming kettle, and the cat between us, and the table laid for tea, Mrs. Williams speculated with interest and hope about those young strangers. Did I notice what badge was on his cap? My eyes were better than hers. She trusted it would be all right for them. They were starting very young. It was better to start young. She looked such a good little soul, that girl. It was pleasant to know that house was let at last. It had been empty too long. It was getting a name. People could not help remembering why it was empty. But young life would make it bright.

"People say things only change, but I like to think they change for the better, don't you? But Williams, he will have it they change for the worse. I don't know, I'm sure. He thinks nothing really good except the old days." She laughed quietly, bending to tickle the cat's ear—"nothing good at all except the old days. Even the wrecks were more like wrecks." She looked at me, smiling.

"As you know," she said, "there's many men who follow the sea with homes in this street, but Williams is so proud and strong-willed. He says he doesn't want to hear about them. What do they know about the sea? You know his way. What do they know about the sea? That's the way he talks, doesn't he? But surely the sea is the same for us all. He won't have it, though. Williams is so vain and determined."

The captain knocked. There was no doubt about that knock. The door surrendered to him. His is a peremptory summons. The old master mariner brought his bulk with dignity into the room, and his wife, reaching up to that superior height, too slight for the task, ministered to the overcoat of the big figure which was making, all unconsciously, disdainful noises in its throat. It would have been worse than useless for me to interfere. The pair would have repelled me. This was a domestic rite. Once in his struggle with his coat the dominant figure glanced down at the earnestness of his little mate, paused for a moment, and the stern face relaxed.

With his attention concentrated and severe even in so small an effort as taking from his broad back a reluctant coat, and the unvarying fixed intentness of the dark eyes over which the lids, loose with age, had partly folded, giving him the piercing look of a bird of prey; and the swarthiness of his face, massive, hairless, and acutely ridged, with its crown of tousled white hair, his was a figure which made it easy to believe the tales one had heard of him when he was the master of the *Oberon*, and drove his ship home with the new season's tea, leaving, it is said, a trail of light spars all the way from Tientsin to the Channel.

The coat was off. His wife had it over her arm, and was regarding with concern the big petulant face above her. She said to him: "Number Ten is let at last. They're a young couple who have got it. He's a sailor."

The old man sat down at a corner of the table, stooped, and in one handful abruptly hauled the cat off the rug, laying its unresisting body across his knees, and rubbing its ribs with a hand that half covered it. He did not appear to have heard what he had been told. He did not look at her, but talked gravely to the fire. "I met Dennison today," he said, as if speaking aloud to himself, in surprise at meeting Dennison. "Years since I saw him," he continued, turning to me. "Where was it now, where was it? Must have been Canton River, the year he lost his ship. Extraordinary to find Dennison still afloat. Not many of those men about now. You can go the length of the Dock Road today and see nothing and meet nobody."

He looked again into the flames, fixedly, as though what he really wanted was only to be found in them. His wife was at his elbow. She, too, was watching them, still with his coat over her arm. She spoke aloud, though more to herself than to us. "She seemed such a nice little woman, too. I couldn't see the badge on his cap."

"Eh?" said the old man, throwing the cat back to the floor and rounding to his wife. "What's that? Let's have tea, Mrs. Williams. We're both dreaming, and there's a visitor. What are you dreaming about? You've nothing to dream about."

There was never any doubt, though, that the past was full and alive to him. There was only the past. And what a memory was his! He would look at the portrait of his old clipper, the *Oberon*—it was central over the mantel-shelf—and recall her voyages, and the days in each voyage, and just how the weather was, what canvas she carried, and how things happened. Malabar Street vanished. We would go, when he was in that mood, and live for the evening in another year, with men who have gone, among strange affairs forgotten.

Mrs. Williams would be in her dream, too, with her work-basket in her lap, absently picking the table-cloth with her needle. But for us, all we knew was that the *Cinderella* had a day's start of us, and the weather in the Southern Ocean, when we got there, was like the death of the world. I was aware that we were under foresail, lower topsails, and stay-sails only, and they were too much. They were driving us under, and the *Oberon* was tender. Yes, she was very tricky. But where was the *Cinderella*? Anyhow, she had a day's start of us. Captain Williams would rise then, and stand before his ship's picture, pointing into her rigging.

"I must go in and see that girl," said the captain's wife once, when we were in the middle of one of our voyages.

"Eh?" questioned her husband, instantly bending to her, but keeping his forefinger pointing to his old ship; thinking, perhaps, his wife was adding something to his narrative he had forgotten.

"Yes," she said, and did not meet his face. "I must go in and see her. He's been gone a week now. He must be crossing the Bay, and look at the weather we've had. I know what it is."

I did then leave our voyage in the past for a moment, to listen to the immediate weather without. It was certainly a wild night. I should get wet when I left for home.

"Ah!" exclaimed the puzzled captain, suddenly enlightened, with his finger still addressing the picture on the wall. "She means the man down the street. An engineer, isn't he? The missis calls him a sailor." He continued that voyage, made in 1862.

There was one evening when, on the home run, we had overhauled and passed our rivals in the race, and were off the Start. Captain Williams was serving a tot all round, in a propitiatory act, hoping to lower the masts of the next astern deeper beneath the horizon, and to keep them there till he was off Blackwall Point. He then found he wanted to show me a letter, testimony to the work of his ship, which he had received that voyage from his owners. Where was it? The missis knew, and he looked over his shoulder for her. But she was not there.

They must have been the days to live in, when China was like that, and there was all the East, and such ships, and men who were seamen and navigators in a way that is lost. As the old master mariner, who had lived in that time, would sometimes demand of me: What is the sea now? Steamers do not make time, or lose it. They keep it. They run to schedule, one behind the other, in processions. They have nothing to overcome. They do not fail, and they cannot triumph. They are predestined engines, and the sea is but their track. Yet it had been otherwise. And the old man would brood into the greater past, his voice would grow quiet, and he would gently emphasize his argument by letting one hand, from a fixed wrist, rise, and fall sadly on the table, in a gesture of solemn finality. He was in that act, early one evening, while his wife was reading a newspaper; and I had risen to go, and stood for a moment silent in the thought that these of ours were lesser days, and their petty demands and trivial duties made of men but mere attendants on uninspiring process.

Serene Mrs. Williams, reading her paper, and not in our world at all, at that moment struck the paper into her lap, and fixed me with surprise and shock in her eyes, as though she had just repelled that mean print in a malicious attempt at injury. Her husband took no notice. She handed me the paper, with a finger on a paragraph. "The steamer *Arab*, which sailed on December 26 last for Buenos Aires, has not been heard of since that date, and today was 'posted' as missing."

I remembered then a young man in uniform, with a rakish cap, trying to find a key while a girl was laughing at him. As I left the house I could see in the dusk, a little down the street, the girl standing at her gate. The street was empty and silent. At the end of it the lamp-lighter set his beacon.

IX
In a Coffee-Shop

With a day of rain, Dockland is set in its appropriate element. It does not then look better than before, but it looks what it is. Not sudden April showers are meant, sparkling and revivifying, but a drizzle, thin and eternal, as if the rain were no more than the shadow cast by a sky as unchanging as poverty. When real night comes, then the street lamps dissolve ochreous hollows in the murk. It was such a day as that; it was not night, for the street lamps were not alight. There was no sound. The rain was as noiseless as the passage of time. Two other wayfarers were in the street with me. One had no right there, nor anywhere, and knew it, slinking along with his head and tail held low, trailing a length of string through the puddles. The other, too, seemed lost. He was idling as if one street was the same as another, and on that day there was rain in all. He came towards me, with his hands in his pockets and his coat collar up. He turned on me briskly, with a sudden decision, when he drew level. Water dripped from the peak of his cap, and his clothes were heavy and dark with it. He spoke. "Mister, could ye give me a hand up? I've made a mess of it." His cheerful and rather insolent assurance faltered for a moment. He then mumbled: "I've been on the booze y'understand." But there was still something in his tone which suggested that any good man might have done the same thing.

It is not easy to be even sententious with the sinful when an open confession robs us of our moral prerogative, so I only told him that it seemed likely booze had something to do with it. His age could have been forty; but it was not easy to judge, for the bridge of his nose was a livid depression. Some accident had pushed in his face under the eyes, giving him the battered aspect of ancient sin. His sinister appearance would have frightened any timid lady if he had stopped her in such a street, on such a day, with nobody about but a lost dog, and the houses, it could be supposed, deserted, or their inmates secluded in an abandonment to misery. And, taking another glance at him, I thought it probable, from the frank regard of the blue and frivolous eye which met mine, that he would have recognized timidity in a lady at a distance, and would have passed her without seeing her. Uncertain whether his guess in stopping me was lucky, he began pulling nervously at a bleached moustache. His paw was the colour of leather. Its nails were broken and stained with tar.

"Can't you get work?" I suggested. "Why don't you go to sea?"

This deliberately unfair question shook his upright confidence in himself, and perhaps convinced him that he had, after all, stopped a fool. He took his cap off, and flung a shower from it—it had been draining into his moustache—and asked whether I did not think he looked poor enough for a sailor.

Then I heard how he came to be there. Two days before he had signed the articles of the steamship *Bilbao*. His box had gone aboard, and that contained all his estate. The skipper, to be sure of his man, had taken care of his discharge book, and so was in possession of the only proof of his identity. Then he left the shipping office, and met some friends.

Those friends! "That was a fine girl," he said, speaking more to the rain than to me. "I never seen a finer." I began to show signs of moving away. "Don't go, mister. She was all right. I lay you never seen a finer. Look here. I reckon you know her." He plunged an eager hand into an inner pocket. "Ever heard of Angel Light? She's on the stage. It's a fact. She showed me her name herself on a programme last night. There y'are." He triumphed with a photograph, and his gnarled forefinger pointed at an exposed set of teeth under an extraordinary hat. "Eh, ain't that all right? On the stage, too. Met her at the corner of Pennyfields."

It was still raining. He flung another shower from his cap. I was impatient, but he took my lapel confidentially. "Guv'nor," he said, "if I could find the swab as took my money, I lay I'd make him look so as his own mother 'ud turn her back on him. I would. Ten quid."

He had, it appeared, lost those friends. He was now seeking, with varying emotions, both the girl and the swab. I suggested the dock and his ship would be a better quest. No, it was no good, he said. He tried that late last night. Both had gone. The policeman at the gate told him so. The dock was there again this morning, but a different policeman; and whatever improbable world the dock and the policeman of midnight had visited, there they had left his ship, inaccessible, tangled hopelessly in a revolving mesh of saloon lights and collapsing streets. Now he had no name, no history, no character, no money, and he was hungry.

We went into a coffee-shop. It stands at the corner of the street which is opposite the *Steam Packet* beerhouse. You may recognize the place, for it is marked conspicuously as a good pull-up for carmen, though then the carmen were taking their vans steadily past it. The buildings of a shipwright's yard stand above it, and the hammers of the yard beat with a continuous rhythmic clangour which recedes, when you are used to it, till it is only the normal pulse of life in your ears. The time was three in the afternoon. The children were at school, and alone the men of the iron-yard made audible the unseen life of the place. We had the coffee-shop to ourselves. On the counter a jam roll was derelict. Some crumpled and greasy newspapers sprawled on the benches. The outcast squeezed into a corner of a bench, and a stout and elderly matron appeared, drying her bare arms on her apron, and looked at us with annoyance. My friend seized her hand, patted it, and addressed her in terms of extravagant endearment. She spoke to him about that. But food came; and as he ate—how he ate!—I waited, looking into my own mug of tepid brown slop at twopence the pint. There was a racing calendar punctuated with dead flies, and a picture in the dark by the side of the door of Lord Beaconsfield, with its motto: "For God, King, and Country"; and there was a smell which comes of long years of herrings cooked on a gas grill. At last the hungry child had finished scraping his plate and wiping his moustache with his hands. He brought out a briar pipe, and a pouch of hairy skin, and faded behind a blue cloud. From behind the cloud he spoke at large, like a confident disreputable Jove who had been skylarking for years with the little planet Earth.

At a point in his familiar reminiscences my dwindling interest vanished, and I noticed again, through the window, the house fronts of the place I knew once, when Poplar was salt. The lost sailor himself was insignificant. What was he? A deck hand; one who tarred iron, and could take a trick at the wheel when some one was watching him. The place outside might have been any dismal neighbourhood of London. Its character had gone.

The tap-tapping on iron plates in the yard next door showed where we were today. The sailor was silent for a time, and we listened together to the sound of rivets going home. "That's right," said the outcast. "Make them bite. Good luck to the rivets. What yard is that?" I told him.

"What? I didn't know it was about here. That place! Well, it's a good yard, that. They're all right. I was on a steamer that went in there, one trip. She wanted it, too. You could put a chisel through her. But they only put in what they were paid for, not what she wanted. The old *Starlight*. She wouldn't have gone in then but for a bump she got. Do you know old Jackson? Lives in Foochow Street round about here somewhere. He's lived next to that pub in Foochow Street for years and years. He was the old man of the *Starlight*. He's a sailor all right, is Jackson.

"The last trip I had with him was ten months ago. The *Starlight* came in here to the West Dock with timber. She had to go into dry-dock, and I signed on for her again when she was ready. This used to be my home, Poplar, before I married that Cardiff woman. Do you know Poplar at all? Poplar's all right. We went over to Rotterdam for something or other, but sailed from there light, for Fowey. We loaded about three thousand tons of china clay for Baltimore.

"The sea got up when we were abreast of the Wolf that night, and she was a wet ship. 'We're running into it,' said old Jackson to the mate. I was at the wheel. 'Look out, and call me if I'm wanted.'"

The man pushed his plate away, and leaned towards me, elbows on the table, putting close his flat and brutish face, with his wet hair plastered over all the brow he had. He appeared to be a little drowsy with food. "Ever crossed the Western ocean in winter? Sometimes there's nothing in it. But when it's bad there's no word for it. There was our old bitch, filling up for'ard every time she dropped, and rolling enough to shift the boilers. We reckoned something was coming all right. Then when it began to blow, from dead ahead, the old man wouldn't ease her. That was like old Jackson. It makes you think of your comfortable little home, watching them big grey-backs running by your ship, and no hot grub because the galley's flooded. The Wolf was only two days behind us, and we had all the way to go. It was lively, guv'nor. The third night I was in with the cook helping him to get something for the men. They'd been roping her hatches. The covers were beginning to come adrift, y'understand. The cook, he was slipping about, grousing all round. Then she stopped dead, and the lights went out. Something swept right over us with a hell of a rush, and I felt the deck give under my feet. The galley filled with water. 'Christ, she's done,' shouted the cook.

"We scrambled out. It was too dark to see anything, but we could hear the old man shouting. The engines had stopped. I fell over some wreckage." The sailor stroked his nose. "This is what it did.

"Next morning you wouldn't have known the old *Starlight*. All her boats had gone, and she had a list to port like a roof. You wanted to be a bird to get about her. The crowd looked blue enough when they saw the falls flying around at daylight, and only bits of boats. It was a case. Every time she lay down in the trough, and a sea went over her solid, we watched her come up again. She took her time about it.

"The engineers were at it below, trying to get her clear. They had the donkey going. In the afternoon we sighted a steamer's smoke to westward. She bore down on us. I never seen anything I liked better than that. Then the Chief came up, and I saw him talking to the old man. The old man climbed round to us. 'Now, lads,' he said, 'there's a Cunarder coming. But the engineer says he reckons he's getting her clear of water. What about it? Shall I signal the liner, or will you stand by her?'

"We let the Cunarder go. I watched her out of sight. We hung around, and just about sunset the Chief came up again. I heard what he said. 'It's overhauling us fast, sir,' he said to the old man. The old man, he stood looking down at the deck. Nobody said anything for a spell. Then a fireman shot through a companion on all fours, scrambled to the bulwarks, and looked out. He began cursing the sun, shaking his fist at it every time it popped over the seas. It was low down. It was funny to hear him. 'So long, chaps,' he said, and dropped overside.

"We waited all night. I couldn't sleep, what with the noise of the seas running over us, and waiting for something to happen. It was perishing cold, too. At sun-up I could see she might pitch under at any time. She was about awash. The old man came to me and the steward, and said: 'Give the men all the gin they'll drink. Fill 'em up.' Some of 'em took it. I never knew a ship take such a hell of a time to sink as that one.

"I sighted the steamer, right ahead, and we wondered whether the iron under us would wait till she come. We counted every roller that went over us. The other steamer was a slow ship all right. But she came up, and put out her boats. We had to lower the drunks into them. I left in the last boat with the old man. 'Jim,' he said, looking at her as we left her, 'she's got no more than five minutes now. I just felt her drop. Something's given way.' Before we got to the other ship we saw the *Starlight's* propeller in the air. Right on end. Yes. I never seen anything like that—and then she just went . . ."

The sailor made a grimace at me and nodded. From the shipwright's next door the steady, continuous hammering in the dry-dock was heard again, as though it had been waiting, and were now continuing the yarn.

X
Off-Shore

1

For weeks our London days had been handmade with gas and oil. It was a winter of the kind when the heaven of the capital is a brown obscurity not much above the highest reached by the churches, and a December more years before the War then it would be amusing to count. There was enough of the sun in that morning to light my way down Mark Lane, across Great Tower Street to Billingsgate. I was on my way to sea for the first time, but that fortune was as incredible to me as the daylight. And as to the daylight, the only certainty in it was its antiquity. It was a gloom that was not only because the year was exhausted, but because darkness was falling at the end of an epoch. It was not many years before the War, to be a little more precise, though then I was unaware of the reason of the darkness, except common fog.

Besides, why should a Londoner, and even an East-Ender whose familiar walls are topped by mastheads, believe in the nearness of the ocean? We think of the shipping no more than we do of the paving stones or of the warnings of the pious. It is an event of the first importance to go for a first voyage, though mine was to be only by steam-trawler to the Dogger Bank; yet, as the event had come to me so late, I had lost faith in the omens of London's foreshore, among which, at the bottom of Mark Lane, was an Italian baking chestnuts over a coke fire. The fog, and the slops, and the smell by Billingsgate, could have been tokens of no more than a twopenny journey to Shepherd's Bush. I had believed in the signs so little that I had left my bag at a railway station, miles away.

Three small steamers, the size of tugs, but with upstanding bows and a sheer suggesting speed and buoyancy, were lying off the fish market, and mine, the *Windhover*, had the outside berth. I climbed over to her. Blubber littered her iron deck, and slime drained along her gutters. Black grits showered from her stack. The smell from her galley, and the heat from her engine-room casing, were challenging to a stranger. It was no place for me. The men and porters tramping about their jobs knew that, and did not order me out of their way. This was Billingsgate, and there was a tide to be caught. They hustled me out of it. But the skipper had to be found, for I must know when I had to come aboard. A perpendicular iron ladder led to her saloon from a hatch, and through unintelligence and the dark I entered that saloon more precipitously than was a measure of my eagerness, picked myself up with a coolness which I can only hope met with the approval of some silent men, watching me, who sat at a table there, and offered my pass to the man nearest me.

It was the mate. He scrutinized the simple document at unnecessary length, and with a gravity that was embarrassing. He turned up slowly a large and weather-beaten sadness, with a grizzled moustache that curled tightly into his mouth from under a long, thin nose which pointed at me like a finger. His heavy eyes might have been melancholy or only tired, and they regarded me as if they sought on my face what they could not find on my document. I thought he was searching me for the proof of my sanity. Presently he spoke: "Have you *got* to come?" he said, and in a gentle voice that was disconcerting from a figure so masculine. While I was wondering what was hidden in this question, the ship's master entered the saloon briskly. He was plump and light. His face was a smooth round of unctuous red, without a beard, and was mounted upon many folds of brown woollen scarf, like an attractive pudding on a platter. He looked at me with amusement, as I have no doubt those lively eyes, with their brows of arched interest, looked at everything; and his thick grey hair was curved upwards in a confusion of interrogation marks.

He chuckled. "This is not a passenger ship," he said. "That will have to be your berth." He pointed to a part of the saloon settee which was about six feet forward and above the propeller. "A sou'-wester washed out our only spare cabin, comin' in. There you are." He began to climb the ladder out of it again, but stopped, and put his rosy face under the lintel of the door. "You've got twenty minutes now. Get your luggage aboard."

My bag was where it could not be reached in twenty minutes. Roughing it may have its humours, but to suffer through it, as I was aware I must, if I stayed, would more than outweigh the legitimate interest of a first voyage, except for heroic youth with its gift of eternal life. Simple ignorance, as usual, made me heroic. I went on deck, and found the steward sitting on a box, with a bucket of sprats before him, tearing off their heads, and then throwing the bodies contemptuously into another bucket. The ends of his fingers and thumbs were pink and bright, and were separated from the remainder of his dark hands by margins of glittering scales. He compared to me, as he beheaded the fish, the girls of Hull and London. But what I knew of the girls of but one city was so meagre in comparison that I could only listen to his particulars in silent surprise. It was notable that a man like that, who pulled the heads and guts of fish like that, should have acquired a knowledge so peculiar, so personal, of the girls of two cities. While considering whether what at first looked like the mystery of this problem might not be in reality its clue, I became aware of another listener. Its lean and dismal length was disproportionate to that small ship. It had on but dungarees and a singlet, and the singlet, because of the length of the figure, was concave at the stomach, where, having nothing to rest upon, it was corrugated through the weight of a head made brooding by a heavy black beard. Hairy wrists were thrust deeply into the pockets to hold up the trousers. The dome of its head was as bald and polished as yellow metal. The steward introduced me to the Chief Engineer. "Yon's a dirty steward," returned the Chief simply.

"Clean enough for this ship," said the Steward.

"Aye," sighed the engineer, "aye!"

"Have you been to the Queen's Hall lately?" asked the Chief of me. "I should like to hear some Beethoven or Mozart tonight. Aye, but we're awa'. It'll be yon sprats." He sighed his affirmative again in resignation, and stood regarding the steward bending over the pails on the deck. "What make ye," he asked, "of this war between the Japs and Russia? Come awa' doon, and have a bit talk. I canna' look at that man's hands and argue reasonable. It'd no be fair to ye."

We could not have that argument then, for I had so little time to go ashore and purchase what necessaries could be remembered while narrowly watching the clock. I was astride the bulwarks again when the *Windhover* was free of her moorings. There was a lack of deliberation and dignity in this departure which gave it the appearance of improvisation, of not being the real thing. I could not believe it mattered whether I went or not. My first voyage had, that is, those common circumstances which always make our crises incredible when they face us, as if they had met us by accident, in mistake for some one else. The bascules of the Tower Bridge went up, this time to let out me. Yet that significant gesture, obviously made to my ship, was watched with an indifference which was little better than cynicism. What was this city, past which we moved? In that haze it was only the fading impress of what once was there, of what once had overlooked the departure of voyagers, when on memorable journeys, in famous ships. Now it had almost gone. It had seen its great days. There was nothing more to watch upon its River, and so it was going. And was an important voyage ever made by one who had forgotten his overcoat? The steward rose, raised his bucket of fish offal, emptied it overboard, and went below. It was not easy to believe that such a voyage could come to anything, for London itself was intangible, and when we got past those heavier shades which were the city, and were running along the Essex marshes, though there was more light, there was nothing to be seen, not even land substantial enough to be a shadow. There was only the length of our own ship. Our pilot left us, and we felt our way to the Lower Hope, a place I could have accepted if it had not been on the chart, and anchored.

Night came, and drove me below to the saloon, where we made five who sat with the sprats, now fried, and mugs of tea before us. The saloon was the hollow stern, a triangle with a little fireplace in its base, and four bunks in its sides. Its centre was filled with a triangular table, over which, pendent from the skylight, was an oil-lamp in chains. A settee ran completely round the sides, and on that one sat for meals, and used it as a step when climbing into a bunk. The skipper cheerily hailed me. "As you're in for it, make yourself comfortable. Sorry we can't do more than give you the seat to sleep on. But the chief thing in this ship is fish. Try some sprats."

"Aye, try yon sprats," invited the Chief. "Ye'll get to like them well, in time." After the fish there was cards, in which I took no hand, but regarded four bent heads, so intent they might have been watching a ritual of magic which might betray their fate; and, above those heads, motionless blue cirrus clouds of tobacco smoke wreathing the still lamp. The hush was so profound that we could have been anchored beyond the confines of this life.

2

What the time was next morning when I woke I do not know, for the saloon was too dark to show the clock, over the fireplace. But the skylight was a pale cube of daylight, and through it I could see a halyard quivering and swaying, apparently in a high wind. My bench was in a continuous tremor.

We were off again. Somebody appeared at the doorway, a pull of cotton waste in his hand, and turned a negroid face, made lugubrious by white lines which sweat had channelled downwards through its coal dust. It looked at me, this spectre with eyes brilliant yet full of unutterable reproach, saw that I was awake, and winked slowly. It was the second engineer. He said it was a clear morning. We had been under way an hour. He had got sixty revolutions now. He then receded into the gloom beyond; but materialized again, or, to be exact, the white stare of two disembodied eyes appeared, and the same voice said that it had won seventeen and six-pence last night, but there was something funny about the way the skipper shuffled cards.

Feeling as though I were in one piece, I got up, made my joints bend again, and went on deck. Our ship, tilting at the immobile world, might have upset the morning, which was pouring a bath of cold air over us. The overcoat of the skipper, who was pacing the bridge, flapped in this steady current. A low coast was dim on either hand, hardly superior to the flawless glass of the Thames. By the look of it, we were the first ever to break the tranquillity of that stream. We ourselves made scarcely a sound; we could have been attempting a swift, secret and, so far, unchallenged escape. The shores unfolded in a panorama without form. Once we spun past an anchored ship, or what had been a ship before the world congealed to this filmed crystal, but now it was a frail ghost shrouded in the still folds of diaphanous night, its riding lights following us like eyes. In the horny light of that winter dawn we overhauled, one after another, the lamps of the Thames estuary, the Chapman, the Nore, and the Mouse, and dropped them astern. We made a course east by north to where the red glints of the Maplin and Gunfleet lights winked in their iron gibbets. Above the shallows of the Burrows Shoal the masts projected awry of the wreck of a three-masted schooner, and they could have been the fingers of the drowned making a last clutch at nothing.

We got abreast of Orfordness, and went through the gate of the North Channel upon a wide grey plain. We were fairly at sea. We were out. The *Windhover*, being free, I suppose, began to dance. The sun came up. The seas were on the march. Just behind us was London, asleep and unsuspecting under the brown depression of its canopy; and as to this surprise of light and space so near to that city, so easily entered, yet for so long merely an ancient rumour, an old tale of our streets to which the ships and the wharves gave credence—how shall the report of it sound true? Not at all, except to those who still hold to a faith, through all foul times, in the chance hints of a better world.

A new time was beginning in such a world. There was a massive purple battlement on the sea, at a great distance, the last entrenchment of night; but a multitude of rays had stormed it, poured through clefts and chasms in the wall, and escaped to the *Windhover* on a broad road that was newly laid from the sky to this planet. The sun was at one end of the road, and we were at the other. There were only the two of us on that road. On our port beam the shadow which was East Anglia became suddenly that bright shore which is sometimes conjectured, but is never reached.

The *Windhover* drove athwart the morning, and her bows would ride over the horizon to divide it, and then the skyline joined again as she sank below it. We were beginning to live. I did not know what the skipper would think of it, so I did not cheer. Sometimes the sea did this for me, making a loud applause as it leaped over the prow. The trawler was a good ship; you could feel that. She was as easy and buoyant as a thoroughbred. She would take a wave in a stride. I liked her start of surprise when she met a wave of unexpected speed and strength, and then leaped at it, and threw it, white and shouting, all around us. It was that part of a first voyage when you feel you were meant to be a navigator. To stand at the end of the bridge, rolling out over the cataracts roaring below, and to swing back, and out again, watching the ship's head decline into a hollow of the seas, and then to clutch the saddle as she reared with a sudden twist and swing above the horizon, and in such a vast and illuminated theatre, was to awake to a new virtue in life. We were alone there. There were only comets of smoke on the bright wall of the sky, of steamers out of sight.

At sunset we made Smith's Knoll Light, and dropped the land. The cluster of stars astern, which was a fleet of Yarmouth herring boats at work, went out in the dark. I had, for warmth and company in the wheel-house on the bridge, while listening to the seas getting up, only signals from Orion and the Great Bear, the glow of the pipe of the silent fellow at the wheel, and the warm shaft of light which streamed from somewhere in the ship's body and isolated the foremast as a column of gold. There was the monody, confident but subdued, the most ancient song in the world, of invisible waters. Sometimes there was a shock when she dropped into a hollow, and a vicious shower whipped across the glass of the wheel-house. I then got the sad feeling, much too soon, that the inhospitable North was greeting us. It is after sundown at sea, when looking through the dark to the stars, listening to sounds that are as though ancient waters were still wandering under a sky in which day has not been kindled, seeking coasts not yet formed, it is in such nights that one's thoughts are of destiny, and then the remembrance of our late eager activities brings a little smile. There being no illumination in the wheel-house but the restricted glow from the binnacle, this silent comment of mine on man and his fate caused the helmsman no amusement. "I hope you are bringing us luck this trip," said the sailor to me. "Last trip we got a poor catch. I don't know where the fish have got to." Somewhere, north-east about two hundred miles, was the fleet which, if I were the right sort of mascot to the Windhover, we should pick up on the evening of the next day.

3

When I left the wheel-house to go below, it was near midnight. As I opened the heavy door of the house the night howled aloud at my appearance. The night smelt pungently of salt and seaweed. The hand-rail was cold and wet. The wind was like ice in my nose, and it tasted like iron. Sometimes the next step was at a correct distance below my feet; and then all that was under me would be swept away. I descended into the muffled saloon, which was a little box enclosing light and warmth partially submerged in the waters. There it smelt of hot engine-oil and stale clothes. I got used to the murmuring transit of something which swept our outer walls in immense bounds, and the flying grind of the propeller, and the bang-clang of the rudder when it was struck . . . and must have gone to sleep. . . .

When I woke, it was because the saloon in my dreams had gone mad. Perhaps it had been going mad for some time. Really I was not fully awake—it was four in the morning, the fire was out, and violent draughts kept ballooning the blanket over me—and in another minute I might have become quite aware that I had gone to sea for the first time. It was my bench which properly woke me. It fell away from me, and I, of course, went after it, and my impression is that I met it halfway on its return journey, for then there came the swooning sensation one feels in the immediate ascent of a lift. When the bench was as high as it could go it overbalanced, canting acutely, and, grabbing my blanket, I left diagonally for a corner of the saloon, accompanied by some sea-boots I met under the table. As I was slowly and carefully climbing back, the floor reversed, and I stopped falling when my head struck a panel. The panel slid gently along, and the mate's severe countenance regarded me from inside the bunk. I expected some remonstrance from a tired man who had been unfairly awakened too soon. "Hurt yourself?" he asked. "It's getting up outside. Dirty weather. Take things easy."

I took them as easily as perhaps should be expected of a longshoreman. There was no more sleep, though no more was wanted. By putting out my hand to the table I managed to keep where I was, even when, in those moments of greatest insecurity, the screw was roaring in mid-air. Our fascinating hanging lamp would perform the impossible, hanging acutely out of plumb; and then, when I was watching this miracle, rattle its chain and hang the other way. A regiment of boots on the floor—I suppose it was boots—would tramp to one corner, remain quiet for a while, and then clatter elsewhere in a body. Towards daybreak the skipper appeared in shining oilskins, tapped the barometer, glanced at me, and laughed because my pillow—which was a linen bag stuffed with old magazines—at that moment became lower than my heels, and the precipitous rug tried to smother me. I enjoyed that laugh.

Later still, I saw that our dark skylight was beginning to regain its sight. Light was coming through. Our lunatic saloon lamp was growing wan. I ventured on deck. When my face was no more than out of the hatch, what I saw was our ship's stern upturned before me, with our boat lashed to it. It dropped out of view instantly, and exposed the blurred apparition of a hill in pursuit of us—the hill ran in to run over us—and in that very moment of crisis the slope of wet deck appeared again, and the lashed boat. The cold iron was wet and slippery, but I grasped it firmly, as though that were an essential condition of existence in such a place.

The *Windhover*, too, looked so small. She was diminished. She did not bear herself as buoyantly as yesterday. Often she was not quick enough to escape a blow. She looked a forlorn trifle, and there was no aid in sight. I cannot say those hills, alive and deliberate on all sides, were waves. They were the sea. The dawn astern was a narrow band of dead white, an effort at daybreak suddenly frustrated by night, but not altogether expunged. The separating black waters bulked above the dawn in regular upheavals, shutting out its pallor, and as incontinently collapsed again to release it to make the *Windhover* plainer in her solitude.

The skipper waddled briskly aft, and stood beside me. He put his nose inside the galley. "I smell coffee," he said. His charge reared, and pitched him against the bulwarks. "Whoa, you bitch," he cried cheerfully. "Our fleet ought not to be far off," he explained. "Ought to see something of them soon." He glanced casually round the emptinesss of the dawn. He might have been looking for some one with whom he had made an appointment at Charing Cross. He then backed into the hatch and went below. The big mate appeared, yawned, stooped to examine a lashed spar, did not give the sunrise so much as a glance, did not allow the ocean to see that he was even aware of its existence, but went forward to the bridge.

The clouds lowered during the morning, and through that narrowed space between the sea and the sky the wind was forced at a greater pace, dragging rain over the waters. Our fleet might have been half a mile away, and we could have gone on, still looking for it. The day early surrendered its light, a dismal submission to conditions that had made its brief existence a failure. It had nearly gone when we sighted another trawler. She was the *Susie*. She was smaller than the *Windhover*. We went close enough to hail the men standing knee-deep in the wash on her deck. It would not be easy to forget the *Susie*. I shall always see her, at the moment when our skipper began to shout through his hands at her. She was poised askew, in that arrested instant, on a glassy slope of water, with its crest foaming above her. Surge blotted her out amid-ships, and her streaming forefoot jutted clear. She plunged then into the hollow between us, showing us the plan of her deck, for her funnel was pointing at us. Her men bawled to us. They said the *Susie* had sighted nothing.

Our engine-bell rang for us to part company. Our little friend dropped astern. She seemed a poor little thing, with a squirt of steam to keep her alive in that stupendous and hurrying world. A man on her raised his arm to us in salute, and she vanished.

4

The talk of our skipper, who began to be preoccupied and abrupt veered to the subject of Jonah. We should now have been with our fleet, but were alone in the wilderness, and any course we took would be as likely as another. "This hasn't happened to me for years," he apologized. He stared about him, tapping the weather-dodger with his fingers, and whistled reflectively. He turned to the man at the wheel. "Take her east for an hour, and then north for an hour," and went below.

Day returned briefly at sunset. It was an astonishing gift. The clouds rapidly lifted and the sky cleared, till the sea extended far to a bright horizon, hard and polished, a clear separation of our planet and heaven. The waves were still ponderous. The *Windhover* laboured heavily. We rolled over the bright slopes aimlessly. She would rear till the forward deck stuck up in front of us, then drop over, flinging us against the dodger, and the shock would surround her with foam that was an eruption of greenish light.

The sun was a cold rayless ball halved by the dark sea. The wall of heaven above it was flushed and translucent marble. There was a silver paring of moon in a tincture of rose. When the sun had gone, the place it had left was luminous with saffron and mauve, and for a brief while we might have been alone in a vast hall with its crystalline dome penetrated by a glow that was without. The purple waters took the light from above and the waves turned to flames. The fountains that mounted at the bows and fell inboard came as showers of gems. (I heard afterwards it was still foggy in London.) And now, having made all I can of sunset and ocean, and a spray of amethysts, jacinths, emeralds, zircons, rubies, peridots, and sapphires, it is no longer possible for me to avoid the saloon, the thought of which, for an obscure reason, my mind loathed.

And our saloon, compared with the measure of the twilight emptiness now about us, was no bigger than the comfort a man feels amid mischance when he remembers that he is still virtuous. The white cloth on its table, I noticed, as I sat down, was contaminated by a long and sinful life. But the men round it were good and hearty. I took my share of ham and fish on the same plate, and began to feel not so hungry as before. I was informed that ashore we are too particular about trifles, because we have the room for it, but on a trawler there is not much room. You have to squeeze together, and make do with what is there, because fish is the most important passenger. My hunk of bread was placed where the cloth bore the imprint of a negro's hand. The mugs of tea were massive, and sweetish (I could smell that) with condensed milk. Did I want my tea? I noticed there were two men between me and the exit, and no room to pass. The room was hot. The bench was rising and falling. My soul felt pale and faintly apprehensive, compelling me, now I was beset, to take hold of it firmly, and to tell it that this was not the time to be a miserable martyr, but a coarse brute; and that, whether it liked it or not, I was going to feed at once on fish, ham, and sickly liquor, and heaven help us if it failed me before these sailors. It made no response, being a thin nonconformist soul, so I had to leave it, and alone I advanced on the food. As so often happens, the conquest was a little less hard than it appeared to be. I progressed, though slowly, and at last was sufficiently disengaged from my task to count the minutes moving at their funeral pace to the end of the meal. The heat of the room mounted. The movements of the ship continued to throw my stomach against the edge of the table.

My companions, however, were in no hurry to move. They discussed, among other things, Hull, and its unfortunate system of sanitation. While this gossip, which was explicit with exuberant detail, was engaging us, I summoned my scientific mind, which is not connected with my soul, to listen to what was being said, and the rest of me was deaf. They went on to tell each other about other trawlers and other crews. Other ships and men, I heard, had most of the luck. "The fish follow some of 'em about," complained the skipper. "I should like to know how it's done."

"They ought to follow us," replied the second engineer. "When I went down to take over this morning, Mac was singing Scotch songs. What more could we do below?"

"It's a grand life," nodded his superior's polished bald head. "Aye, there's guid reason for singing. Sing to yon codfish, y'ken."

The skipper looked at the engineer in doubtful innocence. "Well, I wish singing would do it," he said gravely. "I don't know. How do you account for some fellows getting most of the luck? Their ships are the same, and they don't know any more."

Mac shook his head. "The owners think they do. There's their big catches, y'ken. Ye'll no convince owners that the sea bottom isna' wet and onsairten."

The rosy face of the skipper became darker, and there was a spark in his eyes. This was unfair. "But dammit, man, you don't mean to say the owners are right? Do these chaps know any more? Look at old Rumface, old Billy Higgs. Got enough women to make him hate going into any port. Can't be happy ashore unless he's too drunk to know one woman from another. What does he do? Can't go to sea without taking his trawler right over all the fish there is. Is that his sense? Ain't God good to him? Shows him the fish every time."

The engineer stood up, bending his head beneath a beam, crooking an elbow to consider one hairy arm. "Ah weel, I wouldna call it God. Ye canna tell. Man Billy has his last trip to make. Likely he'll catch fish that'd frighten Hull. Aye."

The skipper moved impatiently, made noises in his throat, rose, and both went out. The mate, who had been chewing and looking at nothing all the time, chuckled.

The mate pulled off his big boots, and climbed into his bunk. The steward cleared the table. I had the saloon to myself, and tried to read from a magazine I extracted from my pillow. The first story was rollicking of the sea, and I have never seen more silly or such dreary lies in print. And the others were about women, magazine women, and the land, that magazine land which is not of this earth. The bench still heaved, and there was a new smell of sour pickles. I think a jar had upset in a store cupboard. Perhaps I should feel happier in the wheel-house. It was certain the wheel-house would not smell of vinegar, boots, and engine oil. It would have its own disadvantages—it would be cold and damp—and the wind and seas on the lively deck had to be faced on the way to it. The difficulty there is in placing the second course on London's cosy dinner-tables began to surprise me.

Our wooden shelter, the wheel-house, is ten feet above the deck, with windows through which I could look at the night, and imagine the rest. I had, to support me, the mono-syllabic skipper and a helmsman with nothing to say. I saw one of them when, drawing hard on his pipe, its glow outlined a bodyless face. The wheel chains rattled in their channels. There was a clang when a sea wrenched the rudder. I clung to a window-strap, flung back to look upwards through a window which the ship abruptly placed above my head, then thrown forward to see wreaths of water speeding below like ghosts. The stars jolted back and forth in wide arcs. There were explosions at the bows, and the ship trembled and hesitated. Occasionally the skipper split the darkness with a rocket, and we gazed round the night for an answer. The night had no answer to give. We were probably nearing the North Pole. About midnight, the silent helmsman put away his pipe, as a preliminary to answering a foolish question of mine, and said, "Sometimes it happens. It's bound to. You can see for ye'self. They're little things, these trawlers. Just about last Christmas—wasn't it about Christmas-time, Skipper?— the *Mavis* left the fleet to go home. Boilers wrong. There was one of our hands, Jim Budge, who was laid up, and he reckoned he'd better get home quick. So he joined her. We were off the Tail of the Dogger, and it blew that night. Next morning Jim's mate swore Jim's bunk had been laid in. It was wet. He said the *Mavis* had gone. I could see the bunk was wet all right, but what are ventilators for? Chance it, the *Mavis* never got home. A big sea to flood the engine-room, and there she goes."

5

After the next daybreak time stood still—or rather, I refused to note its passage. For that morning I made out the skipper, drenched with spray, and his eyes bloodshot, no doubt through weariness and the weather, watching me from the saloon doorway. I did not ask any questions, but pretended I was merely turning in my sleep. It is probably better not to ask the man who has succeeded in losing you where you are, particularly when his eyes are bloodshot and he is wondering what the deuce he shall do about it. And greater caution still is required when his reproachful silence gives you the idea that he thinks you a touch of ill-luck in his enterprise. My companions, I believe, regretted I had not been omitted. I tried, therefore, to be inconspicuous, and went up to seclude myself at the back of the boat on the poop, there to understudy a dog which is sorry it did it. Not adverse fate itself could show a more misanthropic aspect than the empty overcast waste around us. It was useless to appeal to it. It did vouchsafe us one ship that morning, a German trawler with a fir tree lashed to her deck, ready for Christmas morning, I suppose, when perhaps they would tie herrings to its twigs. But she was no good to us. And the grey animosity granted us three others during the afternoon, and they were equally useless, for they had not sighted our fleet for a week. All that interested me was the way the lookout on the bridge picked out a mark, which I could not see, for it was obscured where sea and sky were the same murk, and called it a ship. Long before I could properly discern it, the look-out behaved as though he knew all about it. But it was never the sign we wanted. We had changed our course so often that I was beginning to believe that nobody aboard could make a nearer guess at our position than the giddy victim in blindman's-buff. A sextant was never used. Apparently these fishermen found their way about on a little mental arithmetic compounded of speed, time, and the course. That leaves a large margin for error. So if they felt doubtful they got a plummet, greased it, and dipped it overboard. When it was hauled up they inspected whatever might be sticking to the tallow, and at once announced our position. At first I felt sceptical. It was as though one who had got lost with you in London might pick up a stone in an unknown thoroughfare, and straightway announce the name of that street. That would be rather clever. But I discovered my fishermen could do something like it.

Our skipper no longer appeared at meals. He was on the bridge day and night. He acted quite well a pose of complete indifference, and said no more than: "This has not happened to me for years." He repeated this slowly at reasonable intervals. But he had lost the nimble impulse to chat about little things, and also his look of peering and innocent curiosity. As now he did not come to our table, the others spoke of Billingsgate carriers, such as ours, which had driven about the Dogger till there was no more in the bunkers than would take them to Hull to get more coal. From the way they spoke I gathered they would crawl into port, in such circumstances, without flags, and without singing. This gave my first trip an appearance I had never expected. Imagination, which is clearly of little help in geography, had always pictured the Dogger as a sea where you could hail another trawler as you would a cab in London. A vessel might reasonably expect to find there a fish-trunk it had left behind. But here we were with our ship plunging round the compass merely expectant of luck, and each wave looking exactly like the others,

But at last we had them. We spoke a rival fleet of trawlers. Their admiral cried through a speaking-trumpet that he had left "ours" at six that morning twenty miles NNE., steaming west. It was then eleven o'clock. Hopefully the *Windhover* put about. We held on for three hours at full speed, but saw nothing but the same waves. The skipper then rather violently addressed the Dogger, and said he was going below. The mate asked what course he should steer. "Take the damned ship where you like," said the skipper. "I'm going to sleep." He was away ten minutes. He reappeared, and resumed his silent parade of the bridge. The helmsman grinned at the mate. By then the wind had fallen, the seas were more deliberate; there came a suffusion of thin sunlight, insufficient and too late to expand our outlook, for the night began to fill the hollows of the Dogger almost at once, and soon there was nothing to be seen but the glimmer of breaking waves.

6

There is nothing to be done with an adventure which has become a misprise than to enjoy it that way instead. What did I care when they complained at breakfast of the waste of rockets the night before? What did that matter to me when the skylight above our morning coffee was open at last, really open? Fine weather for December! Across that patch of blue, which was a peep into eternity, I saw drift a bird as white as sanctity. And did it matter if the imprints on our tablecloth of negroes' thumbs were more numerous and patent than ever, in such a light? Not in the least. For I myself had long since given up washing, as a laborious and unsatisfactory process, and was then cutting up cake tobacco with the rapture of an acolyte preparing the incense. If this was what was meant by getting lost on the Dogger, then the method, if only its magic could be formulated, would make the fortunes of the professional fakirs of happiness in the capitals of the rich. Yet mornings of such a quality cannot be purchased, nor even claimed as the reward of virtue.

On deck it was a regal day, leisurely, immense, and majestic. The wind was steady and generous. The warm sunlight danced. I should not have been surprised to have seen Zeus throned on the splendid summit of the greatest of those rounded clouds, contemplative of us, finger on cheek, smiling with approval of the scene below—melancholy approval, for we would remind him of those halcyon days whose refulgence turned pale and sickly when Paul, that argumentative zealot, came to provide a world, already thinking more of industry and State politics than of the gods, with a hard-wearing theology which would last till Manchester came. For the *Windhover* had drifted into a time and place as innocent of man's highest achievements as is joy of death. The wind and sea were chanting. The riding of the ship kept time to that measure. The vault was turquoise, and the moving floor was cobalt. The white islands of the Olympians were in the sky.

Hour after hour our lonely black atom moved over that vast floor, with nothing in sight, of course, in a day that had been left over from earth's earlier and more innocent time, till a little cloud formed in the north. That cloud did not rise. It blew towards us straight over the seas, rigid and formless; becoming at last a barque under full sail, heading east of south of us. She was, when at a distance, a baffling mass of canvas, from which a square-sail occasionally heliographed. She got abeam of us. Before the clippers have quite gone, it is proper to give grace for the privilege of having seen one, superlative as the ship of romance, and in such a time and place. She was a cloud that, when it mounted the horizon like the others, instead of floating into the meridian, moved over the seas to us, an immutable billow of luminous mist blown forward on the wind. She might have risen at any moment. Her green hull had the sheer of a sea hollow. Her bows pressed continually onward, like the crest of a wave curving forward to break, but held, as though enchanted. Sometimes, when her white mass heeled from us under the pressure of the wind, a red light flashed from her submerged body. She passed silently, a shining phantom, and at last vanished, as phantoms do.

7

When the boots, exploded on the saloon floor by the petulant mate, woke me, it was three of a morning which, for my part, was not in the almanac.

"We're bewitched," the mate said, climbing over me into his cupboard. "I never thought I should want to see our fleet so much."

"Aye," remarked the chief engineer, who came shuffling in then for some sleep, "ye'll find that fleet quick, or the stokers are giving orders. D'ye think a ship is driven by the man at the wheel? No' that I want to smell Hull."

A kick of the ship overturned the fireshovel, and I woke again to look with surprise at so small a cause of a terrible sound, and was leaving the shovel to its fate when it came to life, and began to crawl stealthily over the floor. It was an imperative duty to rise and imprison it. When that was forgotten the steward arrived, and roused me to watch the method of setting a breakfast-table at sea; but I had seen all that before, and climbed out of the saloon. There are moments in a life afloat when the kennel and chain of the house-dog appear to have their merits. The same wash was still racing past outside, and the ship moving along. The halyards were shaking in the cold. The funnel was still abruptly rocking. A sailor was painting the starboard stanchions. A stoker was going forward off duty, in his shirt and trousers, indifferent to the cruel wind which bulged and quivered his thin rags. The skipper was on the bridge, his hands in the pockets of his flapping overcoat, still searching the distance for what was not there. A train of gulls was weaving about over our wake. A derelict fish-trunk floated close to us, with a great black-backed gull perched on it. He cocked up one eye at me when he drew level, crouched for flight, but perhaps saw on my face the reason why I prefer working tomorrow, and contemptuously stayed where he was. Then I noticed the skipper looking back at the bird. He nodded to it, and cried: "There goes a milestone. The fleet is about somewhere." I danced with caution along the treacherous deck, where one day that voyage a sea picked up two men and stranded them on top of the engine-room casing, and got up with the master. He had just ordered the ship to be put over to a trawler in sight. With the seas so swift and ponderous I completely forgot the cold wind in watching the two lively ships being manoeuvred till they were within earshot. When the engines were stopped the steering had to be nicely calculated, or erratic waves brought them dangerously close, or else took them out of call. Our new friend had not seen "our lot," but had left a fleet with an unknown house-flag ten miles astern. We surged forward again.

We steamed for two hours, and then the pattern of a trawler's smoke was seen ahead traced on a band of greenish brilliance which divided the sea from the sky. Almost at once other faint tracings multiplied there. In a few minutes we could make out plainly within that livid narrow outlet between the sea and the heavy clouds a concourse of midget ships.

"There they are," breathed the skipper after a quick inspection through his glasses.

In half an hour we were in the midst of a fleet of fifty little steamers, just too late to take our place as carrier to them for London's daily market. As we steamed in, another carrier, which had left London after us, hoisted her signal pennant, and took over that job.

While still our ship was under way, boats put out from the surrounding trawlers, and converged on us for our outward cargo, the empty fish-trunks. That intense band of light which had first betrayed the smoke of the fleet eroded upwards into the low, slaty roof of nimbus till the gloom was dissolved to the zenith. The incubus vanished; the sun flooded us. At last only white feathers were left in the sky. I felt I had known and loved these trawlers for years. All round us were ships' boats, riding those sweeping seas in a gyrating and delirious lunacy; and in each were two jovial fishermen, who shouted separate reasons to our skipper for "the week off" he had taken.

These boats came at us like a swarm of assailants, swooping downhill on us, swerving, recoiling, and falling away, rising swiftly above us again for a charge, and then careering at us with abandon on the next declivity of glass. A boat would hesitate above us, poised and rocking on the snowy ridge of an upheaval, and vanish as the *Windhover* canted away. Then we rolled towards her, and there she was below us, in a smooth and transient hollow. Watching for their chances, snatched out of luck by skill and audacity, our men fed the clamorous boats with empties; the boxes often fell just at the moment when the open boat was snatched away, and then were swept off. The shouted jokes were broadened and strengthened to fit that riot and uproar. This sudden robust life, following the routine of our subdued company on its lonely and disappointed vigils in a deserted sea, the cheery men countering and mocking aloud the sly tricks of their erratic craft, a multitude of masts and smoking funnels around us swaying in various arcs against a triumphant sky, the clamorous desperation of clouds of wheeling kittiwakes, herring-gulls, black-backed gulls and gannets, and all in that pour of hard and crystalline northern sunlight, was as though the creative word had been spoken only five minutes before. We, and all this, had just come. I wanted to laugh and cheer.

8

There is, we know, a pleasure more refined to be got from looking at a chart than from any impeccable modern map. Maps today are losing their attraction, for they permit of no escape, even to fancy. Maps do not allow us to forget that there are established and well-ordered governments up to the shores of the Arctic Ocean, waiting to restrict, to tax, and to punish us, and that their police patrol the tropical forests. But consider the legends on a chart even of the North Sea, of the world beneath the fathoms—the *Silver Pits*, the *Dowsing Ground*, the *Leman Bank*, the *Great Fisher Ground*, the *Horn Reef*, the *Witch Ground*, and the *Great Dogger Bank*! Strange, that indefinable implication of a word! I remember that, when a child, I was awake one night listening to a grandfather's clock talking quietly to itself in its long box, and a brother sat up in bed and whispered: "Look, the Star in the East." I turned, and one bright eye of the night was staring through the window. Heaven knows into what profundity of ancestral darkness my brothers whisper had fallen, nor what it stirred there, but an awe, or a fear, was wakened in me which was not mine, for I remember I could not explain it, even though, at the time, the anxious direct question was put to me. Nor can I now. It would puzzle a psycho-analyst most assured of the right system for indexing secret human motives to disengage one shadow from another in an ancestral darkness. That is why I merely put down here the names to be found on a chart of the North Sea, and say no more about it, being sure they will mean nothing except to those to whom they mean something. Those words, like certain moonbeams, which stir in us that not ourselves which makes for righteousness, or lunacy, combine only by chance. The combination which unlocks the secret cannot be stated, or it would not work. When there is a fortuitous coincidence of the magic factors, the result is as remarkable to us as it is to those who think they know us. When I used to stand on London's foreshore, gazing to what was beyond our street lamps, the names on the chart had a meaning for me which is outside the usual methods of human communication. The Dogger Bank!

Here then it was, yet still to be seen only by faith. It was like Mrs. Harris. I had the luck to discover that I should lose nothing through my visit; and every traveller knows how much he gains when the place he has wished to visit allows him to take away from it no less than what he brought with him. The Bank was twenty fathoms under us. We saw it proved at times when a little fine white sand came up, or fleshy yellow fingers, called sponge by the men, which showed we were over the pastures of the haddock. That was all we saw of a foundered region of prehistoric Europe, where once there was a ridge in the valley of that lost river to which the Rhine and Thames were tributaries. Our forefathers, prospecting that attractive and remunerative plateau of the Dogger, on their pilgrimage to begin making our England what it is, caught deer where we were netting cod. I almost shuddered at the thought, as though even then I felt the trawl of another race of men, who had strangely forgotten all our noble deeds and precious memories, catching in the ruin of St. Stephen's Tower, and the strangers, unaware of what august relic was beneath them, cursing that obstruction to their progress. Anyhow, we should have the laugh of them there; but these aeons of time are desperate waters into which to sink one's thought. It sinks out of sight. It goes down to dark nothing.

Well, it happened to be the sun of my day just then, and our time for catching cod, with the reasonable hope, too, that we should find the city still under St. Stephen's Tower when we got back, as a place to sell our catch.

Our empty boxes were discharged. Led by the admiral, the *Windhover*—with the rest of the fleet—lowered her trawl, and went dipping slowly and quietly over the hills, towing her sunken net. The admiral of a fishing-fleet is a great man. All is in his hands. He chooses the grounds. Our admiral, it was whispered to me, was the wizard of the north. The abundant fish-pastures were revealed to him in his dreams. It was my last evening on the Bank. The day had been wonderfully fine for winter and a sea that is notoriously evil. At twilight the wind dropped, the heave of the waters decreased. The scattered fleet, gliding through the hush, carried red, green, and white planets. The ships which lay in the western glow were black and simple shapes. Those to the east of us were remarkable with a chromatic prominence, and you thought, while watching them, that till that moment you had not really seen them. Presently the moon cleared the edge of the sea, a segment of frozen light, and moored to our stern with a quivering, ghostly line.

Coloured rockets sailed upwards from the admiral when he changed his mind and his course, and then the city of mobile streets altered its plan, and rewove its constellation. At midnight white flares burned forward on all the boats. The trawls were to be hauled. Our steam-winch began to bang its cogs in the heavy work of lifting the net. All hands assembled to see what would be our luck. The light sent a silver lane through the night, and men broke through the black walls of that brilliant separation of the darkness, and vanished on the other side. Leaning overside, I could see the pocket of our trawl drawing near, still some fathoms deep, a phosphorescent and flashing cloud. It came inboard, and was suspended over the deck, a bulging mass, its bottom was unfastened, and out gushed our catch, slithering over the deck, convulsive in the scuppers. The mass of blubber and plasm pulsed with an elfish glow.

9

We were homeward bound. The flat sea was dazzling with reflected sunshine, and a shade had to be erected over the binnacle for the man at the wheel. It might have been June, yet we had but few days to Christmas. The noon ceiling was a frail blue, where gauze was suspended in motionless loops and folds. The track of the sun was incandescent silver. A few sailing vessels idled in the North Channel, their sails slack; but we could not see a steamer in what is one of the world's busiest fairways. We ran on a level keel, and there was no movement but the tremor of the engines. We should catch the tide at the Shipwash, and go up on it to Billingsgate and be home by midnight. How foolish it is to portion your future, at sea!

It was when I was arranging what I should do in the later hours of that day, when we were at Billingsgate, that the skipper, staring round the North Channel, said to me: "It looks as though London had been wiped out since we left it. Where's the ships?"

The Maplin watched us pass with its red eye. We raised all the lights true and clear. I went below, and we were talking of London, and the last trains, when the engine-room telegraph gave us a great shock. "Stop her!" we heard the watch cry below.

I don't know how we got on deck. There were too many on the companion ladder at the same time. While we were struggling upwards we heard that frantic bell ring often enough to drive the engine-room people distracted. I got to the ship's side in time to see a liner's bulk glide by. She would have been invisible but for her strata of lights. She was just beyond our touch. A figure on her, high over us, came to her rail, distinct in the blur of the light of a cabin behind him, and shouted at us. I remember very well what he said, but it is forbidden to put down such words here. The man at our wheel paid no attention to him, that danger being now past, and so of no importance. He continued to spin the spokes desperately, because, though we could not see the ships about us, we could hear everywhere the alarm of their bells. We had run at eleven knots into a bank of fog which seemed full of ships. The moon was looking now over the top of the wall of fog, yet the *Windhover*, which, with engines reversed, seemed to be going ahead with frightful velocity, drove into an opacity in which there was nothing but the warning sounds of a great fear of us. I imagined in the dark the loom of impending bodies, and straining overside in an effort to make them out, listening to the murmur of the stream, nervously fanned the fog with my hat in a ridiculous effort to clear it. Twice across our bows perilous shadows arose, sprinkled with stars, yet by some luck they drifted silently by us, and the impact we expected and were braced for was not felt.

I don't know how long it was before the *Windhover* lost way, but we anchored at last, and our own bell began to ring. When our unseen neighbours heard the humming of our exhaust, their frantic appeal subsided, and only now and then they gave their bells a shaking, perhaps to find whether we answered from the same place. There was an absolute silence at last, as though all had crept stealthily away, having left us, lost and solitary, in the fog. We felt confident there would be a clearance soon, so but shrouded our navigation lights. But the rampart of fog grew higher, veiled the moon, blotted it out, expunged the last and highest star. We were imprisoned. We lay till morning, and there was only the fog, and ourselves, and a bell-buoy somewhere which tolled dolefully.

And morning was but a weak infiltration into our prison. A steadfast inspection was necessary to mark even the dead water overside. The River was the same colour as the fog. For a fortnight we had been without rest. We had become used to a little home which was unstable, and sometimes delirious, and a sky that was always falling, and an earth that rose to meet the collapse. Here we were on a dead level, still and silent, with the men whispering, and one felt inclined to reel with giddiness. We were fixed to a dumb, unseen river of a world that was blind.

There was one movement. It was that of the leisurely motes of the fog. We watched them—there was nothing else to do—for a change of wind. A change did not seem likely, for the rigging was hoar with frost, and ice glazed our deck.

Sometimes the fog would seem to rise a few feet. It was a cruel deception to play on the impatient. A mere cork, a tiny dark object like that, drifting along some distance out, would make a focal point in the fog, and would give the illusion of a clearance. Once, parading the deck as the man on watch, giving an occasional shake to the bell, I went suddenly happy with the certainty that I was now to be the harbinger of good tidings to those below playing cards. A vague elevated line appeared to starboard. I watched it grow into definition, a coast showing through a haze that was now dissolving. Up they all tumbled at my shout. They stared at the wonder hopefully and silently. The coast became higher and darker, and the skipper was turning to give orders—and then our hope turned into a wide path on the ebbing River made by cinders moving out on the tide. The cinders passed. We re-entered our silent tomb. There had been no sign of our many neighbours of the night before, but suddenly we heard some dreadful moans, the tentative efforts of a body surprised by pain, and these sounds shaped, hilariously lachrymose, into a steam hooter playing "Auld Lang Syne," and then "Home, Sweet Home." There followed an astonishing amount of laughter from a hidden audience. The prisoners in the neighbouring cells were there after all, and were even jolly. The day thereafter was mute, the yellow walls at evening deepened to ochre, to umber, and became black, except where our riding lights made luminous circles. Each miserable watcher who came down to the saloon that night, muffled and sparkling with frost, to get a drink of hot coffee, just drank it, and went on deck again without a word.

The motes next morning went drifting leisurely on the same light air, interminable. Our prison appeared even narrower. Then once again a clearance was imagined. Our skipper thought he saw a lane along the River, and up-anchored. The noise of our cable awoke a tumult of startled bells.

Ours was a perishable cargo. We were much overdue. Our skipper was willing to take any risk—what a good master mariner would call a reasonable risk—to get home; and so, when a deck hand, on the third morning, with the thawing fog dripping from his moustache, appeared in the saloon with the news that it was clearing a little, the master decided he would go.

I then saw, from the deck of the *Windhover*, so strange a vision that it could not be related to this lower sphere of ours. It could be thought that dawn's bluish twilight radiated from the *Windhover*. We were the luminary, and our faint aura revealed, through the melting veil, an outer world that had no sky, no plane, no bounds. It was void. There was no River, except that small oval of glass on which rested our ship, like a model.

The universe, which that morning had only begun to form in the void, was grouped about us. This was the original of mornings. We were its gravitational point. It was inert and voiceless. It was pregnant with unawakened shapes, dim surprising shadows, the suggestions of forms. Those near to us more nearly approached the shapes we knew in another life. Those beyond, diminishing and fainting in the obscurity of the dawn, were beyond remembrance and recognition. The *Windhover* alone was substantial and definite. But placed about us, suspended in a night that was growing translucent, were the shadows of what might once have been ships, perhaps were ships to be, but were then steamers and sailers without substance, waiting some creative word, shrouded spectres that had left the wrecks of their old hulls below, their voyages finished, and were waiting to begin a new existence, having been raised to our level in a new world boundless and serene, with unplumbed deeps beneath them. There, on our level, we maintained them in their poise with our superior gravity and our certain body, giving them light, being what sun there was in this new system in another sky. Above them there was nothing, and around them was blind distance, and below them the abyss of space. Their lights gathered to our centre, an incoming of delicate and shining mooring lines.

It was all so silent, too. But our incoming cable shattered the spell, and when our siren warned them that we were moving, a wild pealing commenced which accompanied us on the long drift up to Gravesend. There were eight miles of ships: barges, colliers, liners, clippers, cargo steamers, ghost after ghost took form ahead, and then went astern. More than once the fog thickened again, but the skipper never took way off her while he could make out a ship ahead of us. We drifted stern first on the flood, with half-turns of the propeller for steering purchase, till a boatman, whom we hailed, cried that we were off Gravesend. And was there any one for the shore?

There was. I took no more risks. I had been looking for that life-boat. And what a thing it was to have solid paving-stones under one's feet again. There were naphtha flares in the fog, dingy folk in muddy ways, and houses that kept to one place. There was a public-house, too. Outside that place I remembered the taste of everlasting fried fish, and condensed milk in weak tea; and so entered, and corrected the recollection with a glass of port—several glasses, to make sure of it—and that great hunk of plum-cake which I had occasionally seen in a dream. Besides, this was Christmas Eve.

XI
An Old Lloyd's Register

With the sensation that I had survived into a strange and a hostile era that had nothing to do with me, for its affairs were not mine, I was inside a submarine, during the War, talking to her commander. He was unravelling for me the shining complexity of his "box of tricks," as he called his ship. He was sardonic (there was no doubt he was master of the brute he so lightly villified), and he was blithe, and he illustrated his scientific monologue with stories of his own experiences in the Heligoland Bight. These, to me, were like the bedevilments of those dreams from which we groan to awake, but cannot. The curious doings of this new age, I thought as I listened to him, would have just the same interest for me as the relics of an extinct race of men, except for the urgent remembrance that one of the monstrous accidents this child knows of might happen now. That made an acute difference. This was not nightmare, nor ridiculous romance, but actuality. And as I looked at this mocking youngster, I saw he was like the men of that group on the *Queen Mary* who were similarly mocking, for my benefit, but a few weeks before, their expert share in forwarding the work we had given them in this new age; and then where were they? Ships I knew, but not such ships as these, nor such work.

Another officer joined us, an older man, and said this to him was strange navigation. He was a merchant seaman. He had served his time in sailing ships. I asked him to name some of them, having the feeling that I could get back to the time I knew if I could but hail the ghost, with another survivor from the past, of one of those forgotten ships. "Well," he replied, "there was the *Cutty Sark.*"

If he had said the *Golden Hind* I should not have been more astonished. In a sense, it was the same thing. The *Cutty Sark* was in the direct line with the Elizabethan ships, but at the end. That era, though it closed so recently, was already as far as a vague memory. The new sea engines had come, and here we were with them, puzzled and embarrassed, having lost our reasonable friends. I told him I had known the *Cutty Sark*, and had seen that master of hers—a character who went about Poplar in a Glengarry cap— who gave one of her masts (the mizzen, I think) a golden rooster, after he had driven her from Sydney Heads to the Channel to break the record—Captain Woodget. His men said it was like living in a glass house.

I recalled to him that once, when my business was concerned with bills of lading and freight accounts, I was advised to ship four hundred cases to Sydney, New South Wales; and one-half of that consignment, my instructions ran, was to arrive a month before the other. The first lot went in a modern steel barque, the *Cairnbulg*. ("I have seen her," said this submarine officer). More than a fortnight later, being too young to remember that the little *Cutty Sark* had been one of the China tea clippers, I shipped the last half of the consignment in her. But she disordered all the careful plans of the consignees. She got in a fortnight ahead of the *Cairnbulg*.

The effect of that casual recollection on the submarine officer was distinctly unwarlike. This memory, and not his present work, might have been the real thing. He knew Woodget, the man in the Glengarry. He wanted to know more; ever so much more. He mentioned other ships and masters, to induce me. I got the idea that he would let his mind, at least, escape into that time, if only I would help him to let it go. But there was that potent and silent enigma about us. . . .

No such escape for him. We have fashioned other ships, and must use them. What we have conjured up compels us to live with it. But when you do not go to sea you may have what ships you like. There is some but not much interest in the reappearance in the newspapers of the sailing lists; a few of the old names appear again, though new ships bear them. But late at night, when a westerly wind with rain turns for me a neighbouring yew tree into an invisible surge, then it is the fortune of one who remembers such as the *Cutty Sark* to choose different ships and other times. Why not choose them? They were comely ships, and now their time seems fair. Who would care to remember the power and grey threat of a modern warship, or the exotic luxury of a liner of this new era? Nobody who remembers the graciousness of the clippers, nor the pride and content of the seamen who worked them. To aid the illusion of the yew, I have one of those books which are not books, a *Lloyd's Register of Shipping* for 1880, that by some unknown circuitous route found its way from its first owner in Madras to my suburb. It goes very well with the surge of yew, when westerly weather comes to unite them.

I should like to know how that book got to London. Somewhere in it is the name of the ship which carried it. Anyhow, I think I can make out in it the houseflag of that ship. It, was, I believe, one of J. H. Allan's teak-built craft, a forgotten line—the *Rajah of Cochin*, the *Copenhagen*, the *Lincelles*,—though only just before the War, in the South-West India Dock, I met a stranger, a seaman looking for work, who regretted its disappearance, and the new company-owned steamers; for he said they were good ships, "but more than that," he told me, "Allan was an old gentleman who knew his own ships, and knew his men." This stranger said you forget a ship now as soon as you are paid off, "and glad to," and "you don't ever know who owns her, even if there's a strike. Parsons and old maids and Cardiff sharks, I reckon."

Very likely. But what sharks once were in it have all disappeared from my Register. It belongs to those days when, if you went to New Zealand, you had to go by sailer; when the East India Dock had an arcade of jib-booms and bowsprits, with sometimes a varnished shark's tail terminal—the *Euterpe, Jessie Readman, Wanganui, Wazmea, Waimate, Opawa, Margaret Galbraith, Helen Denny, Lutterworth,* and *Hermione*. There were others. What is in these names? But how can we tell? There were personal figureheads, there were shapely forms, each with its own narrative of adventure, there was the undiscovered sea, and there was youth; and these have gone.

It is all very well to say that the names and mere words in this old Register have no more meaning today than a railway time-table of the same date. Hardly to be distinguished in the shadows in some corners of St. Paul's Cathedral from which night never quite goes, there are certain friendless regimental colours. Few of us know now who bore them, and where, and why; but imagine the deserved fate of one who would allow a brutal word to disturb their dust! They mean nothing, except that men, in a world where it is easy to lose faith, treasure the few tokens of faithfulness, courage, and enterprise proved in their fellows; and so those old staffs, to which cling faded and dusty rags, in a real sense support the Cathedral. Poplar once was a parish whose name was more familiar in Eastern seas and on the coasts of the Americas, and stood for something greater and of more value, than the names of some veritable capital cities. That vista down the East India Dock Road from North Street, past the plane trees which support on a cloud the cupola of Green's Chapel, to the gateway of the dock which was built for John Company, was what many would remember as essential London who would pass the Mansion House as though it were a dingy and nameless tavern. At the back of that road today, and opposite a church which was a chapel-of-ease to save the crews of the East Indiamen lying off Blackwall the long walk to Stebonhythe Church, is the public library; and within that building are stored, as are the regimental colours in the Cathedral, the houseflags of those very ships my Register helps me to remember—the tokens of fidelity and courage, of a service that was native, and a skill in that service which was traditional to the parish. Tokens that now are dusty and in their night, understood only by the few who also belong to the past.

There is the houseflag of the *Cutty Sark,* and her sister ships the *Dharwar, Blackadder, Coldstream*—but one must be careful, and refuse to allow these names to carry one-way. There are so many of them. They are all good. Each can conjure up a picture and a memory. They are like those names one reads in spring in a seed-merchant's catalogue. They call to be written down, to be sung aloud, to be shared with a friend. But I know the quick jealousy of some old sailor, his pride wounded here by an unjustifiable omission of the ship that was the one above all others for him, is bound to be moved by anything less than a complete reprint here of the Register. How, for example, could I give every name in the fleet of the White Star of Aberdeen? Yet was not each ship, with her green hull and white spars, as moving as a lyric? Is there in London River today a ship as beautiful as the old *Thermopylae*? There is not. It is impossible. There was the *Samuel Plimsoll* of that line—now a coal hulk at Gibraltar—which must be named, for she was Captain Simpson's ship (he was commodore afterwards), the "merry blue-eyed skipper" of Froude's *Oceana,* but much more than that, a sage and masterful Scot whose talk was worth a long journey to hear.

The houseflag of Messrs. R. and H. Green, in any reference to the ships of Blackwall, should have been mentioned first. There is a sense in which it is right to say that the founder of that firm, at a time when American craft like the Boston clippers of Donald McKay were in a fair way to leave the Red Ensign far astern, declared that Blackwall had to beat those American flyers, and did it. But that was long before the eighties, and when steam was still ridiculed by those who could not see it equalling clippers that had logged fourteen knots, or made a day's run of over three hundred miles. Yet some of Green's ships came down to the end of the era, like the *Highflyer* and the *Melbourne.* The latter was renamed the *Macquarie,* and was one of the last of the clippers to come home to Poplar, and for that reason, and because of her noble proportions, her picture is kept, as a reminder, by many who wish to think of ships and the sea as they were. It is likely that most who live in Poplar now, and see next to its railway station the curious statue of a man and a dog, wonder who on earth Richard Green, Esq., used to be; though there are a few oldsters left still who remember Blackwall when its shipwrights, riggers, sailmakers, and caulkers were men of renown and substance, and who can recall, not only Richard Green, but that dog of his, for it knew the road to the dock probably better than most of those who use it today. Poplar was the nursery of the Clyde. The flags which Poplar knew well would puzzle London now—Devitt and Moore's, Money Wigram's, Duthie's, Willis's, Carmichael's, Duncan Dunbar's, Scrutton's, and Elder's. But when lately our merchant seamen surprised us with a mastery of their craft and a fortitude which most of us had forgotten were ever ours, what those flags represented, a regard for a tradition as ancient and as rigorous as that of any royal port, was beneath it all.

But if it were asked what was this tradition, it would not be easy to say. Its authority is voiceless, but it is understood. Then what is it one knows of it? I remember, on a day just before the War, the flood beginning to move the shipping of the Pool. Eastward the black cliffs lowered till they sank under the white tower of Limehouse Church; and the church, looking to the sunset, seemed baseless, shining with a lunar radiance. Upriver, the small craft were uncertain, moving like phantoms over a pit of bottomless fire. But downstream every ship was as salient as though lighted with the rays of a great lantern. And there in that light was a laden barque, outward bound, waiting at the buoys. She headed downstream. Her row of white ports diminished along the length of her green hull. The lines of her bulwarks, her sheer, fell to her waist, then airily rose again, came up and round to merge in one fine line at the jibboom. The lines sweeping down and airily rising again were light as the swoop of a swallow. The symmetry of her laden hull set in a plane of dancing sun-points, and her soaring amber masts, cross-sparred, caught in a mesh of delicate cordage, and shining till they almost vanished where they rose above the buildings and stood against the sky, made her seem as noble and haughty as a burst of great music. One of ours, that ship. Part of our parish.